THE NONDUAL SHAMAN®

THE NONDUAL SHAMAN®

*A Contemporary Shamanistic Path
& Thoroughgoing Training for Awakening the Self*

Jason Shulman

THE FOUNDATION
FOR NONDUALITY

JASON SHULMAN LIBRARY

The Foundation for Nonduality
Oldwick, New Jersey 08833

Series Editor: Nancy Yielding
Series Managing Editor: Kimberly Burnham
Editorial Counselor: Shelah Stein
Cover and Interior design: Tom Schneider
MS Word mise-en-scène: Jeff Casper

The Nondual Shaman®
Copyright © 2018 by Jason Shulman.
All rights reserved. Printed in the United States of America.
No part of this book may be reproduced or used in any manner
without the express written permission of the publisher
except for the use of brief quotations in a book review.
Nondual Shaman® and Nondual Voyager™ are trademarked terms
and cannot be used without the written permission
of the trademark holder.

ISBN 978-0-9972201-3-1

10 9 8 7 6 5 4 3 2 1

Other works by Jason Shulman

The Kabbalah Monographs:
 The Work of Briah
 [The Set of the World]
 The Master of Hiddenness
 The Configurations

Ecstatic Speech: Expressions of True Nonduality

The MAGI Process: A Nondual Method for Personal Awakening and the Resolution of Conflict

What does reward bring you but to bind you
to Heaven like a slave? (Poetry)

The Instruction Manual for Receiving God

Kabbalistic Healing: A Path to an Awakened Soul

Dedication

To the reluctant and the brave, the subtle and the forthright, to every walker on the spiritual path, shamans from every direction, Zen-sitters and Insight-watchers, beloved Sufis, yogis and yoginis, Kabbalah-learners, psychotherapists, teachers, nondual healers and all the various practitioners of the spirit: May this book be an open door for all and a way to move closer to the fully human: the living quality of changing and unchanging joy.

Contents

Who I Am and What We Are Doing Together xiii

Why I Sometimes Number My Paragraphs xix

Nondual Shamanism Locates its Home in
   Continuity/Density 1

Introduction to Form-Anxiety 41

What World is This? 49

A Single World 57

The Turn 63

Images 67

The Silent Body 75

An Excursion into Quality 85

The Difference Quality Makes 87
      Quality Meditation 90
      Beautiful Creatures 90

Additional Exercises for the Nondual Voyager 93
      Centered Space 95

Pharaonic Postures 101
      Steps for Pharaonic Postures 110

Walking Through the Densities 111
      Steps for Walking Through the Densities 112

Meditation of the Pure Subjective 115
      Walking to the End of the Universe 120

The Sense of Primordial Space 125

The Living and the Dead 133

Exercises, Conditions, Clothing to Try On 147
      Tasting 147

Geography	148
Seeing Through Empty Eyes	149
Solitude: A Consideration	150
What Constellation? A Contemplation	151
The Collage Metaphor	153
The Gift: Making Magic Manifest	161
Returning to the Source of Power	179
The Active Side of Poisoning Ground	191
Phase One	204
Phase Two	204
Phase Three	205
More on Returning to the Source of Power	206
Exercise	209
Dying to the Self	211
Afterword	215
Appendix One: Languages	221
Opening Your Eyes (and Ears, Nose and Toes) in the Territory and What to Do if You Are Different	221
Pattern Language	225
Visual Grammar	228
Skandhas	235
Learning, Finding and Inventing Other Languages	242
Appendix Two: The Astral Realm and What is Real	245
Appendix Three: Reality's Two Sides	261
Appendix Four: The Chain of Thought	271
Coda	279

Who I Am and What We Are Doing Together

So let's start with who I am not. I am not a Bolivian or Peruvian fellow and have not lived among the ancients in the forests of Columbia. I am not from Siberia nor am I a Native American though a First American was once my dream teacher. In this life I am not Tibetan nor Indian nor a member of a secret sect. I am not from Long Island or San Francisco or Rio or Beijing. I am, however, from Brooklyn, and proud of it. I am a student of Kabbalah, Advaita and Zen, especially the Jodo Shinshu or Pure Land sect. I have sat and meditated most all of my life but do not consider myself a traditional Buddhist per se, though I have had several Buddhist teachers and hold an abiding place in my heart for each one of them.

Still, I am a healer and a nondual shaman. What that is exactly, and how I can be a shaman (or "voyager" as I will call it later) without being from a traditional society is the topic of this book.

Traditionally, shamans are people who have learned to enter into altered states of consciousness for the good of their society, either through the ingestion of psychotropic drugs or through long periods of trance-inducing dancing, drumming or ritual (as examples) in order to access non-ordinary states of reality that allow them to bring back knowledge and acts of healing to those they want to help. Often, they are also experts at the pharmacological use of plants as medicine.

The neo-shamanistic and core-shamanistic movement of recent years has sought to create a form of shamanism that is no longer tied to indigenous cultures but instead tries to find the essential ingredients in traditional shamanism and mold them for modern cultures that are no longer tied to the forest or field.

My approach is not neo-shamanistic, which is to say, it is not a modernized version of traditional shamanism, which uses tools that were originally used in the context of a traditional society and environment. Nondual shamanism also does not attempt to duplicate the look and feel of indigenous healers—although, like the shamans of old, it does see being a shaman as involving the totality of one's life and not so much as a series of special acts. It is a way of living. It recognizes that the intercourse between heaven and earth, between dimensions and worlds—responding to the eternal need for healing in light of the larger view of the full scale of possible human consciousness—is not the province of traditionally-schooled shamans alone, but of all human beings who are willing to undergo the rigorous and exhilarating training it takes to become this type of voyager in our time and place.

In this form of shamanistic healing, the healer is the main object of my attention since the healer must be "made new" in order to accomplish the work of voyaging. This book seeks to help healers have a new paradigm with which to look at themselves and the world, one that both includes and goes beyond the psychological framework. In this new perspective, we are also interested in healing the paradigm maker, the inherent storyteller, which is to say, our ego itself and how it functions within our emotional and psychic environment.

We have come to a time and place in the world where our narrative-making machinery itself must be healed, because—unhealed—it is not a reliable guide for what reality is and is not. It is buffeted by fashion, the political moment, nostalgia for an imagined golden age and rebellion against the current one. Unhealed, it can be a destructive force. But gathered up in insight and tenderness, it is a force for wholeness—another part of our true nature.

We could say that in order to see reality clearly, and with that clarity, begin to have conversations with the sky and earth, we must heal the healer on a profound and thorough level. We must understand why and how our narrative-making egos work the way they do, and—understanding their hurts—heal them so that they might heal others without passing along unspoken suffering and obstacles to living a truthful and healed life.

The nondual approach, as I outline it here, is the best possible approach I have found to this problem. But, unlike traditional nondual approaches, we do not seek to exile the ego as illusory, useless, or an eternal inhibiting obstacle. Instead, with an abiding belief in nonviolence, we try to heal it so that its true function can be free to operate for the good of all. We include the ego, as well as our imperfections, in our work, mixed with the kindness we need to see this journey through. This is a path of flesh and bones, the hard and the soft. A human path. This is the foundation of the journey, the beginning and end as well.

The work of the nondual shaman or voyager does not concentrate on appearances or methodology in any way that overrides or substitutes for the inner journey we must go on in order to be authentic instruments of healing. It seeks to find a new way, one that emerges from within and not from any concept mirrored from the outside. It seeks a model that respects all healing modalities and techniques but is most interested in what is happening in the healer: the state of consciousness, the degree of wholeness, the readiness to open wide the heart and mind.

It says, in essence, that healing takes place from the truly nondual state, a consciousness that does not consider the absolute perspective to be what nonduality is about, but one that combines the impersonal and the personal, the absolute with the relative—one that does not reject the ego because it is troublesome and inconvenient, but rather seeks to heal it so that it can take its beautiful, rightful place in the constellation that makes up each sentient being.

As we come into awareness and union with the totality of our being, we heal. We heal psychologically, culturally and, because we are no longer expending energy to keep illusions alive, we heal physically as well. And because our healed or true nature is now more available to us, we heal others directly if we choose, through our chosen profession as healers, and indirectly, by our very presence in whatever work we do.

If we add to that the very detailed and explicit knowledge of being a nondual voyager, the methodology that does not replace self-awareness and awakening but is its foundation, we have the opportunity and grace to help in a focused and ongoing manner and to reduce suffering in both small and mighty ways.

This work is shamanistic because—taking a cue from the "old ones"—it teaches us how to dive beneath the appearance of things to find how the appearance of things is really the most divine, whole, or healthy thing we could imagine. It trusts the surface of things as the holographic mirror of even the deepest parts. We are explorers of this single thing, in all its facets and dimensions, diving deeply into the ocean of being.

It does not discriminate between various supposed worlds but uses them all to heal the body and soul and, finally, because this is the true object of all healing in this temporary, lightning-quick world, to make a human being who is healthy enough to love.

These pages do not tell the whole story, but they tell part of it. They set the stage for working through the conceptual field so that the mind is freed to listen to the heart. There are exercises along the way to help the student palpably experience the unitive shamanistic state. But it will also be important for the discriminating student to notice those places that are blank, as in "but how do I do this?" Often, I show you how to do this, but often I am pointing you in the direction of learning with a teacher.

The type of learning I am suggesting here is not traditional in the Western sense: you cannot learn to be a nondual shaman or voyager from facts alone. There is an old Kabbalistic story of a young Hasid who travelled to see a great rabbi. Upon his return, his friends said to him "So, how did he say the morning prayer? And did you listen as he expounded the Torah? And did you see his illumination and closeness to God when he broke the bread and said the prayer on Sabbath?" The young Hasid answered: "No. I didn't look for those things. I went to see him tie his shoes."

This young man knew enough to even consider that the great rabbi tying his shoes might be a holographic guidepost that would show him what holiness looked like in daily life.

This book is all about daily life. It is not about journeys to other dimensions (though they show up . . .), nor is it about special guides or creatures (though they might show up too . . .). It is about daily life and how we, as highly trained, dedicated seekers and workers in the world of spirit, as imperfectly impeccable beings, can help. Help in the here and now. Help ourselves—because helping is the greatest illumination and liberation possible—and help others, because after all, they are really ourselves in disguise.

The book begins with a description of *continuity/density*, which is the paradigm through which all of our work will be seen and through which it grows. *Continuity/density* describes an alternate perspective to the compartmentalization and conceptualization of different realms and instead treats reality as a single *continuity* with varying degrees of vividness.

It will also introduce you to a path that leads toward a life of self-responsibility, one built on healing ourselves of our most ingrained and unconscious defenses and bringing them to the surface so that they are no longer exiled but part of the family of who we are. This is how we reduce the power they possess when they are unconscious arbiters of our life. This is also how we begin to stop unconsciously passing our unhealed pain on to others.

The power of the metaphor of *continuity/density* flows through the shaman's entire life and work. It creates a seat from which the aspiring shaman can meditate through the whole of life with deeper acceptance and tenderness than is usually possible. It makes the work of healing our neuroses possible and redefines what healing our self and others actually looks like. It is a way of loving the world and simultaneously making the whole world, the seen and unseen parts, a physical experience. It is something our wonderful bodies and nervous systems were created to do.

This material is designed to free you from limiting thoughts or, better yet, to let you see your omnipresent limiting thoughts clearly so that you are not caught by them as frequently, so that you do not always believe that these negative mental utterances are actual pictures of the truth.

Ultimately, a shaman is someone who loves the world. A shaman for our time, city-time, psychological-time, technological-time, and world-nervous-system-time, must go deeply within in a new and fresh way. Psychological insight alone will not suffice, nor will spiritual investigation without egoic acceptance and transformation suffice. Imitation alone cannot help. But because each person has within themselves the seeds of everything they need, which only require the proper amount of darkness, rain, and time to germinate, the proper husbandry this book offers can help send you on your way.

This is the purpose of this book. It is not a substitute for direct contact with a teacher but is a living teaching itself, pointing the way to the next step.

Please enjoy the book. It is a book not so much of what to do but how to be. Ask questions, first of yourself and then of others. Be diligent and faithful, kind and thoughtful. Don't give up. Ever.

Jason Shulman
Truro, 2018

Why I Sometimes Number My Paragraphs

1. Because I see each sentence as a proposition and not prose, something to be worked at, worked on, and worked through and with. With prose, our mind goes into a conventional mode, skimming parts, grouping words together so that we can get the sense quickly and easily. We miss the sound. And, as the great Jewish prayer of the Shema tells us, the realization of God's Singleness (read here: the unifying Wholeness of Reality . . .) starts with the word *shema*, which means "Listen!" Here, I want the reader to linger over each paragraph and find its power. To hear its Voice. I first saw this methodology used by the Viennese philosopher Ludwig Wittgenstein. Of course, he learned it from someone else and we're still trying to find the fellow that started the whole thing . . .

2. The concern of this book is the voyager himself or herself and the transformation the voyager must go through in order to be a small home for the Infinite. Read this book both casually and with deep attention, flowing through whole sections and lingering on each passage. It's organized more like a scroll than a typical book, more like a stream than something that depends on the turning of pages. One idea or practice leads to another in the river-like movement that best exemplifies true learning. This river-ish movement embodies both the logic of the river's shores and the logic of the river itself as it circulates from place to place, from state to state, at once

quiet and hardly moving and at other times rapid enough to dissolve stone. We are the shoreline and the river, the quiet waters and the dissolving ones. Make the most of it.

3. You will notice that there are many marginal comments. This stylistic layout, though lost to us now or formatted as footnotes instead of marginalia or "shoulder notes" as they are sometimes called, has a long and honored history. They were intended to make the printed text a living experience, allowing the reader to glance back and forth between the text and comments about the text. Sometimes they were used for navigation as in, "here is a new section," but sometimes they reflected the author's further thoughts or even opposition to their own text. I have added a special type of marginal note labeled **IYI**, which I have lifted intact from the brilliant, late author David Foster Wallace. IYI means: "If you are interested." They are further thoughts that you can read or skip as you see fit. Skipping them will not interfere with the flow of the text. Reading them might enlighten you further or send you into the woods from which you will need to find your own way out. (Though sometimes being lost in the woods is a great idea…)

The hidden world has its clouds and rain, but of a different kind.
Its sky and sunshine are of a different kind.
This is made apparent only to the refined ones:
those not deceived by the seeming completeness of the ordinary world.

— *Jalal ad-Din Muhamman Balkhi (Rumi)*

If the world is infinite, no order is real. The only things that can be put in order are those with precise limits. We can look for the momentary utility of an order, but not its veracity. The world is a subjective representation that can organize itself in infinite ways. It is proper to look for the order that causes us the least suffering.

— *Alejandro Jodorowsky*

When you are at this place, there is just one grass, there is just one form; there is understanding of form and beyond understanding of form; there is understanding of grass and beyond understanding of grass. Since there is nothing but just this moment, the time being is all the time there is. Grass being, form being, are both time. Each moment is all being, each moment is the entire world. Reflect now whether any being or any world is left out of the present moment.

— *Zen Master Dogen*

Man, being the last creature, is a unity, an image of the Unique. And the violet of the field is equally a unity in the image of the Unique, who, Himself, is indefinable, save by all the unities of all the possible types of the creation.

— *R. A. Schwaller de Lubicz*

What he does not know forms just as much a part of an individual's life as what he knows. What he has not done is just as important as what he has done. What he will be able to do one day forms part of what he is in the midst of doing. What he has been and what he has not been, what he is and what he is not, what he will be and what he will not be all make up equal parts of his world.

— *Alejandro Jodorowsky*

Nondual Shamanism Locates its Home in *Continuity/Density*

1. The fundamental perspective of the nondual voyager/shaman,* in all aspects of the work he or she does, is based on the understanding of *continuity/density*.

2. While ordinary consciousness can be creative, subtle and insightful, the consciousness of *continuity/density* represents a new level of perception, and also of living in the world.

3. Rather than supplanting or doing away with ordinary, consensual consciousness, *continuity/density* includes our ordinary awareness and skills but goes far beyond the assumptions embedded in quotidian consciousness—many of which we are not even aware of. We could say that the view from *continuity/density* actually reveals the inherent limitations of everyday consciousness and shows us something new and vast.

4. *Continuity/density* reveals a truer picture of how the world fits together as a single, unified place and because of that has major implications for how the nondual voyager lives and heals themselves and others.

5. The word *continuity* acknowledges several truths. First, that the world is entirely connected.

---

* The terminology "shaman" and "voyager" are used interchangeably in this book. I often prefer "voyager" because it gently reminds us that a new paradigm of shamanism is being introduced.

6. The connection between all things can be understood on two levels. Conceptually, it is easy to understand that nothing exists in isolation. Every rock or tree, manufactured thing or even feeling or emotion is part of a chain of causation, a context, a web that is completely connected with myriad other things. *Continuity* says: "Everything depends upon something else for its very existence. Nothing stands alone."

7. If we could diagram the connections between even a single object—and by "object" I mean a *tangible* thing (such as a chair, for example) or a seemingly *intangible* thing (such as a thought or feeling), we would have a web-like diagram of immense proportions connected over vast quantities of time and space. This is the first understanding.

8. The second understanding is less intellectual or conceptual and more felt directly—often wordlessly—by our bodies. We notice it at certain times when everything we see seems to fit together into a seamless web. It is often accompanied by a sense of awe or beauty, a sense of connectedness that we cannot put words to. It seems both ungraspable yet palpable. And, interestingly enough, it seems to reside in the physical world rather than some abstract metaphysical sphere.

9. So, this sunset, this newborn, this wonderful painting, this music, this silence, and so on, often breaks through a sort of haze or sleepiness in our consciousness and brings up a feeling we might call *love*, which in this context is not so much an emotion as a state

of being open, of feeling settled, of things being "right."

10. All this is to say that this *continuity* finds its home in the created things of this world, in every object—in the sense I mentioned before.

11. We will call all of these created things, tangible and seemingly intangible, *densities*.

12. So *continuity/density* gives voice to the fact that this sense of completeness and wholeness, which is the *continuity*, is tied to these *densities*.

13. And going further, that this *continuity*, formless and invisible, must have *density* as its partner, and that these two, rather than being a "cause and effect," arise together, a single thing that makes a wholeness large enough to manifest as an indescribable connectedness, which resides in each particular, in each *density*, in each created thing.

14. *Continuity* and *density* are co-dependently arising. They arise together and only together like wave and ocean, like light and shadow, background and foreground, yellow and gold.

15. We will go into this in more depth later in this book.

16. Eventually, through the work of nondual voyaging, the voyager lives in the consciousness of *continuity/density*, which is to say, a world of oneness that

IYI:
Continuity/density exists in the "here and now" and also extends infinitely in all temporal and spatial dimensions. It is a web through all of time and space. So we could say two seemingly opposite things: first, that the "here and now" extends infinitely in all directions, or second, that the "here and now" as one location in time is an irrelevant concept to the voyager who is in *continuity/density*, a consciousness that remarkably is both a-temporal and a-spatial and temporal and spatial in the same moment.

Time begins to enter the picture.

simultaneously has different, separate things.

17. The oneness of the nondual voyager is large enough to encompass every manifestation of the *continuity/density*. The oneness we are interested in is large enough to contain duality just as it is and the voyager just as he or she is.

18. In addition, the nondual voyager begins to understand that everything in the *continuity/density* is *here* and exists in the here and now.

> In the here and now, the presence of a *density* is connected to its vividness or intensity.

19. So, since everything is—from this point of view—in the here and now, we have a relationship that transcends time and space because it *includes all of time and space*. Later on in this book, we will go into more depth about the concept which I call "one world," or "a single world."

20. To understand this more fully, we could say that the voyager sees every density in the world as either more or less vivid or intense.

21. So, for example, as you read this book, your consciousness, focused on what you are reading, makes our interaction right now very vivid or intense.

22. Other people, though you can bring them to mind, are less vivid. In voyaging, we will call this phenomenon "more or less dense."

23. There is a spectrum, in other words, that flows from things that are so not vivid or *dense* as to be invisible, to things that are very vivid or *dense*. In other words, some are

more in focus while others are out of focus as they are in our field of attention or not.

24. The important thing to remember is not only this spectrum of *densities* or intensities, but that all of this is going on *here*, in the here and now.

25. Thus, the tree in front of us is very vivid, while the inner emotional state of our friend might be somewhat less vivid or intense or, as we now say, *dense*.

26. From the point of view of *continuity/density*, all possible levels of creation are present simultaneously—whether they are vivid, dense or not—at any particular moment.

27. Very vivid densities are present to our most ordinary sense of consciousness and physicality while others, which are *less dense*, are almost transparent, vague, gossamer-like and elusive.

28. From ordinary consciousness, the dead, for example, are nonexistent or only existent in memory or memento. From the point of view of *continuity/density*, however, even the dead are present but less vivid, less intense if you will, unless certain conditions—like a special type of attention the nondual voyager cultivates—are fulfilled.

29. These various intensities or *densities* are fluid to the nondual voyager, and will figure into some aspects of voyaging as we journey through the inner and outer worlds—which themselves will be seen to be a single thing, part of the *continuity/density*.

30. Living in a state of consciousness—and therefore a world—in which *continuity/density* is a living fact, is an entirely different experience than living in a state of consciousness that relies solely on a restricted sensory approach to determine what is important or real.

31. Consciousness that models itself only around the subject/object dichotomy, one that essentially decides ahead of time what a sensorially-valid picture of the world will be, limits our ability to interact with realities that do not fall so easily into this valid—but restricted—version of what reality actually is from the vantage-point of *continuity/density*.

32. Our usual psychological awareness is an example of a type of consciousness that does not clearly see that the view we have of reality is a product of *what* or *who* is doing the viewing rather than an objective "fact" or "truth" that has no connection to the *means* by which we know.

33. This usual style of knowing is still looking solely at the *content* of consciousness and not the "content-provider," the one who participates in the generation of content or adds coloration to what is observed or seen or known.

34. Because of this, this type of ordinary awareness does not see the ego as an editorial opinion but only a neutral, receptive organ, which it mistakenly believes sees "the world as it is."

    The ego as an editorial opinion.

35. For the nondual shaman, life is a *continuity*, an indivisible whole divided into separate

manifestations, beings and details, within which he or she can be conscious of more or less vivid or *dense* beings, conditions, questions, answers, journeys, rhythms, assonances and associations.

36. This version of reality is much like Indra's web,* a woven arrangement in which each strand is totally connected to every other strand so that touching one node of the web resonates throughout the entire structure.

37. It is this complete connectivity—which still takes into account differences—that we can use to help other beings and ourselves as voyagers and healers. Everything, in other words, is available in the here and now to the nondual voyager.

38. The voyager is at home in the world of dualities, the world of opposites and different things. The voyager does not need to make them into anything other than what they are.

39. Without the awareness of *continuity/density*, the tools we use to look at the world are personal-perceptual and psychological tools, in which the I-thought—that continually ongoing and fundamental thought that establishes an historical, fixed sense of identity—maintains an invisible presence, but one not noticed by our ordinary consciousness, even though everything revolves around it.

IYI:
The Buddha said that samsara (this world of duality) and nirvana (the world of liberation) are a single thing. Yet, it has become fashionable to choose only the absolute as the desired goal of nonduality. This is a mistake. True nonduality understands that samsara and the absolute, which is to say duality and oneness, arise together, and that nondual understanding is the experience of the simultaneity of both as a palpable, bodily experience.

---

* "Imagine a multidimensional spider's web in the early morning covered with dew drops. And every dew drop contains the reflection of all the other dew drops. And, in each reflected dew drop, the reflections of all the other dew drops in that reflection. And so ad infinitum. That is the Buddhist conception of the universe in an image." Alan Watts

40. This act of "not noticing," which separates the ego from our consciousness, actually results in a sort of negative freedom for the ego, making it a silent, central organizing principle, separated from our awareness. When this is so, the ego can act without restraint or reflection.

41. In other words, when there is still a viewer who is not acknowledged as being part of and *within* the interaction itself, *creating* the situation as well as simply viewing it, the ego-self remains a potentially powerful element of distortion due to the very fact that its presence and actions continue to be invisible and, in this way, not subject to introspection and healing.

42. There is no way for this ego to heal into a reliable and subtle ally without some way to separate us from what we unquestioningly take as our identity. Only when separated by having, as it were, another place to stand, can we see the ego's own state of being, its shape, manner and intentions—all of which were invisible to us as we "lived the life of the ego," without noticing its presence.

43. There is a vital and permanent place for the integrated or healing ego in the voyager's life and work. The awareness of *continuity/density* is a tool for healing this ego that stands so far apart as to lose its connection with its true job as a guide to voyaging itself.

44. The awareness of *continuity/density* is a practice of the nondual voyager that helps bring the awareness of the ongoing ego-self into a continuum with the totality of our

being, rather than letting it stand off to the side as the hidden, omnipotent ringmaster.

45. To do this, we must begin to place the ego itself "on the table" as one of the infinite number of *densities* that arise along with the *continuity*. By doing this, the ego is no longer central but a member of the totality of being.

46. "On the table" is my shorthand for including every *density*, every possible thing in life, in what life *is*, rather than thinking that we *are these things*.

47. So, all objects are "on the table." All feelings, all thoughts, and even our ego, in health, and in need of healing.

48. The nondual voyager will eventually understand that each object that is on this table is not only not rejected or ignored but will be seen as an ally, an intelligent friend in the world of being—even when it is judged to be negative, dissonant or difficult.

49. And since *continuity* and *density* arise together, each *density* will be found to be a doorway into the *continuity* and the *continuity* itself the mother of manifestation.

50. Many years ago, I created a diagram to illustrate the paradox of the spiritual journey, its origins and its resolution:

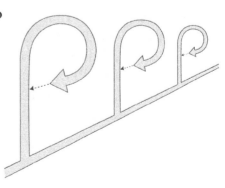

51. This diagram showed the essence of the spiritual journey—indicated by the dotted line which lays out the journey from "where we are" (the arrow-point) to where unity lies (at the end of the dotted line).

52. The irony is that we continue on this path of self-improvement until we begin to realize that we are made of the goal itself, that we need to do something our unhealed egos find counterintuitive, namely, go backward into our origin instead of outward toward an imagined goal, a goal that is really just our self as it is.

53. Yet, this ultimately disappointing journey is a necessity for the deeper, counterintuitive change of direction that brings us out of the vaguely mystical back into the body, our ground of being where true awakening into healing occurs.

54. The increasing ability to be aware of *continuity/density* as an actual reality, felt in the mind and the body, runs parallel to the journey of becoming free of the preconceptions we have built up of who we believe we are.

55. This persona is at first invisible to us. It—with its cast of internal characters, introjections of other people's needs for us to be a certain way, cultural pressures and general miseducation—builds a narrative that hides all of its internal structures from our conscious awareness, the better to convince us that this identity is seamless and real.

56. We act as if we were someone who had a personal identity over which we have ownership, as if this identity were not simply the syntax or context of our historical and social life. We take for granted, in other words, that we are an entity that "owns things," including being the owner of him or herself.

57. To the extent that we are identified with this narrative, we are locked in the personal view of our lives and of life around us, and in this way, miss the depth of connection to ourselves, others and the world we might have if this belief were not so engraved upon our consciousness.

58. Only when our unhealed ego—the somewhat confused keeper of these identities—begins to heal does it allow us to return to a newly useful and deepened life, one in which our now healthier ego no longer insists on maintaining a central position in our psyche.

59. The process of investigation into our narrative, its origins and its functions, automatically creates a sort of spaciousness that allows some of this automatic identification to fall away.

60. As this falling away happens, we can begin to feel connections with the world around us in new and fresh ways.

61. *Continuity/density* offers such a fresh and creative view.

62. From the view of the personal-*alone*, who we are is something separate from the world.

We stand apart and view the scene. This "standing apart" is vital in some way to our internal understanding of being a person who has an identity and agency in the world.

63. This is, of course, a needed skill that we do not need to give up or throw away as we also evolve to a more nuanced and free experience of life.

64. To re-state briefly some of the concepts we covered before, but perhaps in different words, *continuity/density*—as an evolutionary development to our usual consciousness—sees every thing, whether it is a physical object or our sense of identity itself, as simply one of the *densities* that constitute the world. Our thoughts and feelings are *densities*. Our sense of identity, our physical bodies, our relationships—all that we are, all that the world is—are *densities* as well.

65. *Continuity* itself teaches us that everything in the universe is connected. Everything is essentially responsible for the existence of everything else, though it doesn't often look like this on the surface.

66. From this point of view, cause and effect are simultaneous rather than separated, so that a change in one thing affects everything else immediately. Yet, in this non-binary view, cause and effect are also separated in time, so that the connections between things, even if they are immediate, may not be apparent for moments—or centuries.

67. As we are less attached to a single, historical identity with its narrative, but freer to

Understanding *features*.

connect with everything around us, we begin to see that everything in the world is a *feature* of the *continuity*.

68. Whether we are talking about our beliefs (no matter whether they are true or not, evolved or not) or our thoughts (no matter whether they are open and free or closed and limited), they are all *features*.

69. The nature of the *continuity* is that it is filled with *features*. *Features* are not an outgrowth of the *continuity*, something made by the *continuity*, but part of its nature, the way wetness is the nature of rain, or the color yellow, which cannot be separated from gold.

70. Seeing that all of what exists are *features* increases our ability to see widely and freely. It decreases the psychological insistence that everything be regarded personally, as something aimed at the personal self or personally owned. From this viewpoint, even the sense of being personal is a *feature* of this entirely connected world.

71. This allows for a mature form of freedom that is not freedom from but freedom *with*.

72. As I have mentioned before, the nondual voyager is rigorously trained. He or she must evolve in order to do this work. Simply giving various techniques to the voyager-to-be and not nurturing and maturing the limited view and understanding we all have of ourselves, would only create limited voyagers or, in actuality, voyagers who could not voyage—except in fantasy.

> Using another metaphor, we could say continuity and density are the two piers that hold up an arch. Without these piers there could not be a connected and free-standing structure. This "structure" is what we call reality.

73. As we take this process further, the voyager begins to notice that in this seamlessly connected world, a world that is so connected and full that it also allows for distinctions, separation and differences between things, there are a billion, billion gateways to understanding and freedom.

74. As large as freedom is, that is how large the possibilities for freedom are.

75. Put another way, every object in the *continuity* is holy, which is to say, an entry point to the All, a path to deeply holding a *continuity* that includes all *densities* and understanding that *densities* make the *continuity* apprehendable and even possible.

76. True nonduality can never separate these two perspectives.

77. Again, let's re-state another concept in different words: imagine for a moment that we have an empty table before us and that on this table we place all the elements of existence.

78. So, here is my deep desire for spiritual understanding, and here too is my selfishness and small-mindedness. Over here, my parents, and there, evolved and un-evolved thoughts about safety, love, intimacy and so on.

79. In other words, we place everything on the table, and everything on the table—just as it is—is a *feature*.

80. The nondual voyager's attitude toward all of these *features* is to allow them all to exist just as they are.

81. We are depending here on the spiritual truth that everything that is allowed to exist returns to light.

82. This does not mean we give up our agency to change what is not right, to heal what is not healed, but that even this healing is done from the wisdom that comes from allowing each thing to express its true nature, a nature which always has—even if it is in a very distorted form—a desire for light in its center.

83. Further, even our agency, our desire and ability to heal, are "on the table." Nondual voyaging is not about some sort of cartoon "acceptance." We try to change what must be changed because even our desire to do *that* is part of the universe.

84. To return to the diagram we talked about a little while ago, when we look at ourselves and the world as *features*, we are not in a developmental or linear perspective.

85. From a developmental perspective, which is a perspective that lives in sequential time, we must:

    a) Journey toward some spiritual goal;

    b) Realize at some point that we are made of the very thing we are looking for;

    c) Make a counterintuitive move and walk back down toward our root, even if that root contains old sufferings; and finally,

d) Reconnect with our origin.

86. Every movement is movement toward a higher goal.

87. The view from *continuity/density* is not as linear or developmental. The voyager—having gone on this journey of self-discovery and disillusionment previously, now sees that all positions on the arrow and its base are simply *features* and, because of that, are all valid ways of entering the place where voyaging takes place, and are all valid expressions of the Divine.

88. The voyager is *free* to choose and not *compelled* to choose because they are pushed by the ancient winds of the destiny they had to endure during childhood.

89. Seeing everything—from happy to egregious—as *features* allows us to disconnect properly from the personal-*only* view and sink toward wisdom, which is not about being smart or brilliant but about being connected and kind.

90. It is also not about being personal-*alone or* impersonal-*alone,* or relative *or* transcendent separately. Instead, the nondual voyager lives in the place where two worlds touch, like lovers making love, which is to say, creating.

91. An additional point: there is a moment, as we learn to live in this state of mind, that we are not even bothering to *name* all of the *features*. We are not in a trance: we could

call a "pencil" a "pencil" immediately if so asked.

92. But in this non-naming state, this openness and vast panoramic vision, we can encounter *feature's* opposite: *featurelessness.*

Features and featurelessness

93. Both *featurelessness* and *features* give us a wide, unbroken view of life. They do this because, putting everything on the table, so to speak, has the benefit of making our sense of reality less personal. Our imperfections do not spell our doom but, being part of a universal human nature that itself is now on the table, we see that everything can be worked with both kindness and discipline.

94. And a final point: An even more important consequence of perceiving the world as filled with *features* is that the nondual voyager exists firmly and comfortably in a world of duality.

95. In many spiritual paths, opposites are held in order to reconcile them in some form of unity. This is very important and is a large component of healing.

96. But the voyager is not trying to reconcile or reunite opposites at all. This is because from the point of view of *features,* all *densities* are spiritually equal, at least in potential (certain ones might be chosen over others because of the consideration of skillful means at that moment, but not because they are essentially more or less real in some manner.)

The voyager in the world of duality

97. This means that *each opposite* is complete in and of itself, and not only when it is reconciled with its opposite member. We could even say that each *feature* (which is a *density*) is a complete expression of the *continuity* itself.

98. The result of this is that the nondual voyager lives in a completely dynamic environment filled both with the tensions and delight of *things as they are*. This is the arena they live and work in.

99. Having all of these opposites at their disposal, nondual voyagers have many tools at the ready. For example, *wholeness*, that quality spiritual seekers value so much, is simply the opposite pole of something we might call "brokenness." Because the voyager is not seeking to reconcile anything and because all things, which is to say all opposites, have the space in which to exist in their fundamental form, *brokenness* must be one of the *features* of this view.

100. Does *wholeness* heal? Or does *brokenness* heal as well? If the healer insists on some form of wholeness, they might miss the person who needs to be broken before anything can take place. They might not see that habits or thought patterns need to be broken or even that the body must be broken in some manner before something new can come into being. A seven-year illness I went through in my thirties broke me to the extent that I found my path in life through that brokenness.

101. The voyager, living in *continuity/density*, seeing everything within and without as

IYI:
We could say that each pole of an opposite, when viewed and lived as a *feature*, is self-illuminating, which is to say that it shimmers with what the Buddhists call "such-ness." This glimmering arises from the fact that each object, each pole in the duality *is* the *continuity* itself.

features held in *featurelessness*, lives in a world energized by the truth of being. And all of this has direct implications for the way the voyager walks—and works—through life.

102. Living in *continuity/density,* there is "room" for every sort of *density.* The *continuity* is not upset by the addition of any *density.* Instead, we are simply getting a more and more clear picture of reality.

103. The concept (and experience) of *featurelessness* allows us to experience the boundless space that is prepared for every *feature.*

104. This *featurelessness*—which cannot exist without its companion *features*—is what is meant by Emptiness, called *shunyata* by the Buddhists. This emptiness is not so much a concept of "nothingness," but one of "no discursive thinking," thinking that divides the world into bits and pieces. Rather, this is the state of non-conceptuality, which allows the *continuity* of a world filled with *densities* to be revealed.

    IYI:
    The spiritual concept of "emptiness" does not mean nothing is there. Emptiness is simply the view from *featurelessness,* a state in which all conceptual "names" are lost. But, if we look at this state from the viewpoint of *features* themselves, we would have to call this state *fullness.*

105. Paradoxically, this is also a state of completely connected *fullness,* and it is this state of fullness that the nondual voyager relates to, wades into, and dives deeply beneath.

106. These *densities,* these *features,* which are manifestations of the *continuity* in this physical dimension, are the waves of the world.

107. To bring some of this down to the very practical, by building on a foundation of

continuity/density and *feature/featurelessness*, the voyager's view of life in general, and their approach to healing others, becomes more and more relaxed and spacious.

108. As the personal ego heals, its constant quest for safety—even at the cost of creativity and originality—is subdued and we can begin looking for knowledge in the context of healing ourselves and others in an associative, panoramic state that is alive and gently awake. We call this state *bucolic mind*.

    The arising of bucolic mind

109. However, by even using the word "emptiness," we are still seeing this from the ego's point of view, albeit an ego that is integrating back into the whole. There is another way to see this state.

110. *Bucolic* is usually defined as "pastoral, rustic, having to do with shepherds and flocks." In our work it is meant to evoke a kind of stroll through nature, through the *continuity/density*, within a mindset that looks at all in a non-urgent, open way.

111. The voyager with *bucolic mind* is already in touch with the changes *continuity/density* brings to consciousness and has already experienced the relaxation that comes from shifting the personal-*only* view to one in which the ego is not in charge of the journey.

112. We might say that the voyager now walks through the field, with its weeds and stones, trees and fences, sky and water, without knowing what is important or might later be important. Consequently, the voyager in this state is alert to everything without being tense about anything.

> The mastery that is needed here is *no-mastery*, the exquisite surrender to the emptiness beyond characteristics and personality to find the fullness of all creation, a totality that must include characteristics and personality once again.

113. All tension or leftover egoic struggles are placed on the table—or in this case, the field—to be journeyed with along with every other promising encounter. We are in the state of "not knowing, but paying attention." I will discuss what we do pay attention to a little later, in a series of separate chapters.

114. The *bucolic view* is as wide as the field is large. It is not an urgent view. The field—to bucolic mind—is *featureless* but completely filled with interrelationships, intimacies, the whispers between each animal, insect, plant and element.

115. It is a unity with distinct parts, much like a physical field is home to a myriad of interconnections and endless life.

116. At this point, nothing has yet been born as a separate entity. The *continuity* and the *densities* exist together as a single whole, each piece the whole and the whole in each piece, at the same time. The entry-point to the universal is in each particular while each particular evokes the universal.

117. In the world of the nondual voyager, there are things and things and things within an unvarying wholeness.

118. Space is not empty, as we were led to believe, but completely full of the ongoing and dynamic relationships between each piece. There is a steadiness present that is at once unmoving and eternal and in constant motion.

> Opposites are not bereft of life because they are not united with their partner. Instead, each thing shimmers with the light of the continuity. Reality from this viewpoint is spellbinding.

119. As the ego relates to the truths of *continuity/density* and the less personal perspectives of *features* and *featurelessness*, it enters the healing state. Unlike the unhealed ego, which is constantly focused on survival, the healing ego does not focus myopically on a single thing, but chooses from all the shades and differences, dimensions and beings of the universe, from all the available vividness and *densities*, as a choice from among equals, in which one feature is consciously *elevated* over another because it is useful to the task at hand rather than chosen because of the invisible—but omnipresent—program of survival.

120. The nondual voyager is a student of ego-death.

121. We could also be a bit less dramatic and say *ego-integration*, since when a component of any system is integrated and takes its place in the whole, it—for all intents and purposes—disappears. It becomes both *featureless* and simply a *feature* in a world of features.

122. We don't notice the tires of our car when they are new and in good shape and therefore an effortless part of the moving vehicle.

123. When we are feeling healthy, integrated, accepting of all of our *features*, whether good or bad, feeling independent, interdependent and intimate with our environment, we don't notice our egos, that is, they don't exist in our consciousness as a separate, free-standing part. From this vantage point we could describe them as "featureless."

124. We might also say that the nondual voyager does not care about ego-death in this case. Even if we are still afraid of physical death, here the voyager is walking the waterways, gazing at the incoming light, living with the weather, all *features* of this enormous *continuity*.

125. Whether he or she will be liked or disliked for what he or she does is purely secondary. This enlivens the process since this process becomes congruent with the process of life itself. It is simply the way we live.

126. To get to this stage needs practice, and much of it has to do with giving up happiness or sadness, victory and defeat. There is no prior idea of what success—or for that matter, failure—looks like. Yet, happiness occurs, sadness too. One can be happy or sad, all *features* of human life.

127. All *features* are part of the ongoing activity of the universe.

128. Let me quote from a Tibetan text by Yumo Mikyo Dorje, *The Six Lamps*, written around the year 1160, as translated by Christopher Hatchell:

> *Set primordial gnosis nakedly, not clothed in the "animal skin" of conceptuality. Set awareness in its bareness, not spoiling it with minds of clinging and desire. Not creating or altering anything in the mind, set it in an untouched manner. Not following after memories or concepts, set it without chasing or grasping. With little motion in the mind, set it in the great equality. Not stopping the flow of awareness, extend the rope of the innate state.*

129. As evocative—and helpful—as this passage is, we need to head-off any misconception by taking it a step further: Since we are human, and since our human abilities include being in memory and conceptual thinking—to alter and touch, to cling and have desire—and since all of these are *also part of the vast field of wholeness,* the nondual voyager, with his or her truly *bucolic mind,* accepts even these varied and variable states as a valid part of the great unity.

130. The voyager *looks forward to all of it,* knowing in advance that he or she will fail time after time, falling back into the small ego's sense of danger. But even this "failure" is part of the field of victory.

131. This makes the voyager's job even harder, as there is truly no place left to stand that is apart from the whole, no place the ego can set up shop and, glancing backward, say, *look at what I have created.* The shaman-voyager is always "in the mix."

132. Following the example of Tibetan Bon shamans, we can say that we strive to experience an exterior world in which we

consciously avoid the overlay of additional characteristics beyond what is there in front of us.

133. "Exterior world" is an important addition because the nondual shaman-voyager is not a psychological fellow in that he or she is not looking under anything for the truth, but trusting that the truth is everything that is presented and that his or her job is to choose from among these truths.*

> IYI:
> We could also say that the holographic and fractal nature of reality are trusted completely. Thus, the surface *is* the interior. The surface *features*, when trusted in this way, reveal even deeper aspects of what we still call "the interior."

134. But all of these truths must be come to honestly. In other words, we don't choose from among truths with the secret program of keeping ourselves "safe" from the encroachment of unappetizing realizations.

135. Making sure this does not happen under the cover of "nondual shamanism," "voyaging," "wholeness," or "freedom," calls for constant vigilance in the service of honesty.

136. We are never interested in that mythical beast called "perfection." We are simply interested in letting the world—including our own limitations and shortcomings—in. This is what wisdom is made of.

137. So, immersed in the *continuity* of reality, and alert to what is densest at the moment, the voyager brings all of his or her skills to seeing the *physical world* from the point of

---

* The point is not to abandon the psychological dimensions—indeed, we are psychological beings as much as physical beings—but to put even that activity into the perspective of *continuity/density*. It almost goes without saying that our psychological investigation of the structures of our personal identity continues—forever—unabated. The results of this investigation, oxygenated, so to speak, by the understanding of this level of wholeness, makes the results of our insights that much more profound.

view of skills and not from the point of view of some psychologically-based alternative view, one in which the owner of the view, the ego, still stands apart, knowing he or she is safe from utter transformation.

138. In other words, we don't stand apart and make a "shamanistic narrative." We *are the narrative and the storyteller.*

139. In this view the healing ego is the associative web-maker whose job it is to connect all—or better—to see the already-established connections between all things.

140. What is densest is what is at hand, and even this can change at a moment's notice because the voyager is nimble.

141. Nimbleness is a product of freedom—the freedom gained by the practice of accepting failure as success, defeat as victory, of being able to *not prefer one density over another, yet being willing to choose,* to be willing to follow every lead to every dead end, to sit in that dead-end unafraid, to wait, to wander, to regain the world.

142. The commitment to always seeing *density* as a companion to *continuity* is what allows real magic into the world.

143. Nondual voyagers are magicians. But real magic is no conjuror's trick or finesse with illusion. Real magic is the logical end of a life of honest inquiry. In other words, our lifelong passion for walking the spiritual path does lead to something.

> Recognition of the world's true unity is the fertile ground that allows true magic to appear. The nondual voyager can become a true magician, not due to any special powers, but because the world itself, settled down and seen clearly, *is* magic.

144. But this "thing" it leads to is not something "new," something we have never heard of before. Instead, it leads to *ripening*, to maturing. It exists in time and, through time, leads to a new variation of a basic truth.

145. This is in the same way that the logical endpoint of grapes might be a fine wine, achieved by letting the grapes grow, husbanding them correctly, protecting them, learning the skills of wine-making and finally bottling the final product.

146. Through this exterior, time-bound process, the grape shows itself in a new dimension. It reveals an unfolded identity, no better or worse than a fruit grape enjoyed cold from the refrigerator, but simply different, something that could not have been achieved without devotion to time and consciousness.

147. So it is with magic. The real magic is all around us. Now, we are not stating a Hallmark-card bromide as in, *there are miracles all around us*. While this is true, to taste, feel, and even work with this miracle-that-is-already-here takes skill and patience; it takes time for this realization to descend from the feel-good level to a depth of heart that changes our every action.

148. In C. G. Jung's personal investigation of the truth of his soul, he realized that he needed to go into the darkness in order to attain the true magic his soul desired. This darkness is not negative, though it was difficult and, for Jung, often frightening.

149. Here is an extended dialog between Jung ("I") and his soul ("S") regarding an encounter with magic:*

> S: *Do you hear something?*
>
> I: *I'm not aware of anything, what should I hear?*
>
> S: *A ringing.*
>
> I: *A ringing? What? I hear nothing.*
>
> S: *Listen harder.*
>
> I: *Perhaps something in the left ear. What could it mean?*
>
> S: *Misfortune.*
>
> I: *I accept what you say. I want to have fortune and misfortune.*
>
> S: *Well, then, raise your hands and receive what comes to you.*
>
> I: *What is it? A rod? A black serpent? A black rod, formed like serpent—with two pearls as eyes—a gold bangle around its neck. It is not like a magical rod?*
>
> S: *It is a magical rod.*
>
> I: *What should I do with magic? Is the magical rod a misfortune? Is magic a misfortune?*
>
> S: *Yes, for those who possess it.*
>
> I: *That sounds like the sayings of old—how strange you are, my soul! What should I do with magic?*

---

* *The Red Book: A Reader's Edition* © 2009 By the Foundation of the Works of C.G. Jung. Translation © 2009 by Mark Kyburz, John Peck, and Sonu Shamdasani.

S: Magic will do a lot for you.

I: I'm afraid that you're stirring up my desire and misunderstanding. You know that man never stops craving the black art and things that cost no effort.

S: Magic is not easy, and it demands sacrifice.

I: Does it demand the sacrifice of love? Of humanity? If it does, take the rod back.

S: Don't be rash. Magic doesn't demand that sacrifice. It demands another sacrifice.

I: What sacrifice is that?

S: The sacrifice that magic demands is solace.

I: Solace? Do I understand correctly? Understanding you is unspeakably difficult. Tell me, what does this mean?

S: Solace is to be sacrificed.

I: What do you mean? Should the solace that I give or the solace that I receive be sacrificed?

S: Both.

I: I'm confused. This is too dark.

S: You must sacrifice solace for the sake of the black rod, the solace you give and the solace you receive.

I: Are you saying that I shouldn't be allowed to receive the solace of those I love? And should give no solace to those I love? This means the loss of a piece of humanity, and what one calls severity toward oneself and others takes its place.

> S: *That is how it is.*
>
> I: *Does the rod demand this sacrifice?*
>
> S: *It demands this sacrifice.*
>
> I: *Can I, am I allowed to make this sacrifice for the sake of the rod? Must I accept the rod?*
>
> S: *Do you want to or not?*
>
> I: *I can't say. What do I know about the black rod? Who gives it to me?*
>
> S: *The darkness that lies before you. It is the next thing that comes to you. Will you accept it and offer it our sacrifice?*
>
> I: *It is hard to sacrifice to the dark, to the blind darkness—and what a sacrifice!*
>
> S: *Nature—does nature offer solace? Does it accept solace?*
>
> I: *You venture a heavy word. What solitude are you asking of me?*
>
> S: *This is your misfortune, and—the power of the black rod.*
>
> *[The dialogue and discussion goes on for many more pages . . .]*

150. The journey toward magic is a difficult one. Of course, it need not be as difficult or severe as the one Jung had to walk. He was a pioneer without the benefit of others, such as human guides and teachers. Also, these dialogues—and the presences that spoke to him and guided him on his journey of self-realization—were built for him and him alone.

151. Yet, we can learn much here about what needs to be left behind in order to experience this level of the magic of the completely ordinary, when it is a vital—even over-powering force—and not pabulum for the soul.

152. In our context, we can offer a few benchmarks. The foundation of nondual voyaging is the realization of *continuity/density*, and by "realization" I do not mean a one-time experience that overpowers you and changes your life forever. In fact, I mean the complete opposite: it is the commitment to working with this understanding, pushing back if necessary, against the powerful internal currents that insist that either 1) this is not true or 2) that this is dangerous to your soul.

153. We can easily—most easily!—make the mistake of concentrating on either continuity *or* density. This would be an error.

154. *Continuity* alone would err toward the side of the absolute, merging one thing into another. We would—because of the unconscious desire to protect ourselves from the naked energies of the world—begin to see everything as "one," thereby sublimating these potent forces in the name of some phantasmagorical equanimity or something else that was "controllable" or acceptable.

155. *Density* without continuity would elevate personal choice to too high a degree. Here we become connoisseurs of the particular,

reveling in our ability to separate things, to know things that cannot be known, to have subtlety and insight as a matter of the unhealed ego's idea of personal power. This type of personal power degrades us. (There is a type of power that does not. More about that later . . .)

156. But both together lets us begin to understand that all things, conditions, illnesses, successes, failures, sounds and silences, are always present at the same time. Because we accept our egoic self—our "choosing part"—as a valid part of the universe, we can choose which aspect to pay attention to at any given moment. In the same way, we can choose to grieve over our ego's difficulty in being open or companionable or non-competitive, and so on. In the end, as nondual voyagers, we must choose to *practice* each time our omnipresent human difficulties raise their heads.

157. This does not mean that the least dense are made the most dense or the most present, but that our task is to pay attention to the weak signals—as those from the dead or the deadened parts of ourselves—as well as the person next door. All are valid and all are here.

158. This is what makes us safe as voyagers for others. There is no retreat because there is no forward movement. There is no success because there is no failure. This only reveals itself to us as we become mature, as we allow time—without the undue demand for solace—to age us into something fine.

159. We cannot live in this milieu with a high degree of attachment to our separate self. Nor can we live in this milieu if we *have no* separate self. We are the chooser always, using our desires properly, picking up clues the way a magnet picks up iron filings and other bits of metal, weaving the great non-story into narratives that expand—instead of limit—human possibility.

160. Only incarnated, separate beings can do this. Only individuals, precious and separate, are capable of having wide, *bucolic mind*, a mind that is entranced by the magic of the field-as-it-is.

161. We enter *bucolic mind* as we gain the wideness (read: wisdom) to include our own field-as-it-is in the great field of the world.

162. Magic is the world and the world is magic. What this means is that the ego has no magic that lasts but is, at the same time, the magician *and* the magic.

163. But this is a magician who is willing to not know how the trick is done, who focuses instead on the miracle of the existence of magic itself.

164. *At the same time*—because the nondual voyager's life is filled with the practice of holding opposites *until they both reveal their interdependence on one another* and *express their complete independent, self-illuminating nature at the same time*—the voyager knows *exactly* how the magic was done and what made it happen. He or she is not afraid to be a master even though being a master might mean he or she will suffer loneliness

as well as aloneness. I will go into the realization of magic in a later chapter (Making Magic Manifest).

165. The voyager's power is the power of having given up. Of course, I say this with the understanding that we will fail time upon time again in our ability to do this. This is where the commitment to practice saves us from the embarrassment of being human! We bring our humanity and place it on the altar of our commitment. We are the ones who will not stop and, once having stopped, get up and begin again.

166. Curiosity is an important tool for the nondual voyager.

> Curiosity as a tool for paying attention

167. The Diagnostic Process, which is used in Nondual Kabbalistic Healing, is a dialogical approach in which curiosity, as the somewhat neutral attitude of following one's nose while paying attention, has served us well as a tool for relating to others and increasing the intimacy needed to make a correct diagnosis in that discipline.*

---

* The Diagnostic Process is a method—or really a vehicle—that students of Nondual Kabbalistic Healing use to decide which of the many healings they know is the right one for the person they are working with. Unlike characterological approaches—or even psychological ones—the DP is an art form that does not attempt to narrow down the myriad of possibilities in order to find the right diagnosis and therefore the correct approach for the person. Instead, by a process that includes all the opposites the healer finds in the interaction, the correct healing is found not by objectifying the client but by creating a form of intimacy that comes from the totality of the interaction between the healer and the client. This means that all the seeming opposites one encounters on this journey are not only accepted as part of the process but are vital to it. In this way, clarity *and* confusion, excitement *and* boredom, being lost *and* being found, as examples, form a perspective of the client that is deeply enriched in all dimensions rather than one that is concentrated on the pathological issues alone. This radical inclusion even includes the healer's own transference, which the healer has learned to accept through a positive process we call *riding the wave of transference,* which recognizes the precious possibilities inherent in the rectified form of this non-

168. But curiosity from the perspective of *continuity/density* is a somewhat different animal. In the Diagnostic Process, curiosity was still a tool to help us reach a desired end. It was a form of skillful means. But in voyaging, curiosity is now seen not only as a tool or methodology, but as an ingredient in the soup that is *continuity/density* and which *continuity/density* has made. It is another ingredient on the table. It is, in actuality, a type of desire that is built into us, a desire to know, to pay attention in order to know and in order to connect.

169. By using curiosity in this way, we have let go of the skillful, strategic importance of curiosity as a tool that leads to a goal, and allow ourselves instead to experience a form of curiosity that exists with no imagined descendants in mind, no conclusions, no end or even insight, in view.

170. All of our learned strategies for helping have a dualistic version and also one that springs from *bucolic mind* and the ongoing acquaintance with the feeling and tone of *continuity/density*. Now, we no longer use curiosity as a method (or, secretly, hidden even from our own awareness, as a sort of weapon to save us from the unknown!), but are entirely curious. We are propelled by it, made of it. We relate to curiosity *for its own sake* and not for what it will bring. It is a primary motive force.

---

verbal communication. In this way, all is information, and intimacy is established by the broadening of contact with all aspects of the client and healer themselves rather than a characterological narrowing down. The result is the paradoxical movement toward open and nonjudgmental contact, along with the specificity of just the right healing for that occasion.

171. Does this form of curiosity bring something? Does Spring bring Summer? Well, yes and no. Yes, because one thing leads to another since all things are connected. But also no, because all of the *densities* exist at the same moment, in the same instant. When all things also exist at the same time, causality is changed into "every direction at once," and not just confined to the linear awareness of normal, consensual consciousness. When all things exist in the same moment, nothing "brings" anything else. Cause and effect are simultaneous.

> Truly, there is no time. Yet, my wrinkles get deeper every day!

172. This changes what time is and how time is experienced in the act of voyaging.

173. The nondual voyager exists in both times: the linear, sequential (we want to know when it is time for dinner!) and also in the time that occurs all in one moment. Each type of time brings different gifts to the voyager searching for the best way to help someone else.

174. The nondual voyager is also well-acquainted with *dullness*. By *dullness* I mean the sense that remains after the desire for new experiences has been rubbed down and worn away.

175. So, as *stimulation* is no longer the goal, the light of the ordinary shines through. There is beauty, excitement and aliveness.

> Cultivating dullness

176. The nondual voyager is an old dog lying in the sun.

177. Our hunger for experiences that support the unhealed ego's need for self-empowerment as a strategy for survival becomes fainter. It is more and more under control rather than an unconstrained force. We have spaciousness and choice.

178. The internal decision to experience this *dullness* allows the full power of the world to enter us because, in dullness, the ego is the size it should be; it no longer stands in the way of the waves of the world. We no longer need to be empowered in the arena of the single self when we have the entire world to step into.

179. Something that is not "its own size," has a secret agenda, usually one of survival. But please remember: it is not the urge to survive that needs to go away, but its secret demand to remain uniquely alone, not as a *density* among *densities* but as a separate individual alone—a creation not connected to all of creation, which is to say the *continuity*. This is done in a doomed effort to be "safe."

180. True safety—and here I mean spiritual safety, since the physical world cannot be held to be always safe—occurs to the extent that each *density*, each individual thing (or being), is simply itself, honest, singular and naked.

181. To the extent we can allow ourselves to be honest, singular and naked, to that extent we can experience our sense of self and being as a *density* or *spiritual object*. A *density* is always part of the *continuity* and is responsible for the existence of the

continuity itself as part of a mutually co-arising pair. That is where true safety lies, in the unbreakable connection between these two versions of reality.

182. As we feel and experience ourselves as just such a being, our innate dignity becomes apparent because we are not hiding anything but present ourselves as we are.

183. We are our own truth itself, as we are, illuminated because we are as we are, not solipsistic or above it all, but connected to everything, including our true power.

184. When I spoke above about the "waves of the world," I meant both the inner and outer world. In this state of being, inner and outer may present themselves as the harbor and the open sea, but they are artifacts of the same water, dependent upon the nature of the sea for their very life.

185. So, in this state of being, there is only one world. "Inner" and "outer" are simply arrangements or locations of the same material and information.

186. By preparing our *terroir* for nondual voyaging in this way, we learn to accept the impact of the world impartially, which is to say, that though we still have preferences and the personal power—when applicable!—to change things, we are willing to allow the world to contact us impartially, in all its various guises and manifestations.

187. We are willing to be touched.

188. We never know for sure where the magic will surface. We never know if we will like it once it does. We never know if the magic will work or if we will go home to our own meal, contemplating the vast field with its intricately-woven tapestry of what, in our ignorance, we call "successes" and "failures."

189. The ego and all its imperfect reactions to the world are included in this creative collision. In other words: our faults are clearly seen; their effect upon the world is clearly seen; and the world's impact on our own personal desires and preferences, whether they are supported or thwarted, is felt as well.

190. This *dullness*—and its accompanying directness and aliveness—can be learned through a type of work I created some years ago called Form-Anxiety. Please read the passages below and start to practice this important approach to nonduality.

Introduction to Form-Anxiety

Please read this short introduction to Form-Anxiety work and begin practicing this several times per week. Five or ten minutes for each session is sufficient.

1. The infant, coming into this world, experiences the world as what I call "shapes." These shapes are really kinesthetic sensations felt both *within* the child's body *and* as a mediator in the intervening space *between* the child and the mother or father, or even between the child and his or her environment. These shapes have a tendency to change: sometimes they are pleasant to the child and sometimes they are not. And the very existence of this changeability sets up a condition of anxiety for the child. In a sense, each time a shape—or form—changes, the child goes through a kind of death. Anticipation of this recurrent possibility is an anxiety-producing event.

2. So we might say that incarnation itself, the incarnation *into* a form, is the existential basis for *the ending of form*, or death, signified by the constantly changing shapes the child encounters.

3. Form-anxiety, for most of us, continues throughout our entire lives and often is brought to the surface by transitions of every sort.

4. The question comes up of whether this anxiety is *existential* or induced by our parent's dynamic unconscious anxieties.

That is: would a child with parents who completely accepted the child induce form-anxiety? In a sense this question is misleading: the only question we can ask ourselves is: does the *degree* of the parent's anxiety *add to* the existential form-anxiety? The answer is: Yes. All of us have this form-anxiety, which we experience as a reluctance to even feel the sensations in our bodies that are the hallmarks of being alive. In a sense, these streaming energies become the heralds of something frightening, and most of us dull ourselves to even the possibility of feeling them.

5. However, because we do not feel this level of our being, we do not feel life, and because we do not feel life, we are separated from the dynamic possibilities that life evokes in our being. It is essential for the nondual voyager to work directly with this form-anxiety in order to be able to voyage. This will become increasingly clear as we proceed.

6. In the final analysis, *not* feeling form-anxiety means we will not feel *form-preciousness*, which is the final resolution of form-anxiety. (But importantly, *not* the erasure of form-anxiety, which always—paradoxically—remains.)

7. So the first step is to begin to recognize and experience form-anxiety.

8. To do that, we cannot talk about form-preciousness. We cannot do anything that will take us away from the moment, philosophical, intellectual or otherwise.

9. Instead, we are going to begin our practice of form-anxiety by doing this:

10. We will sit, with our eyes open, comfortably, but not slouched or stiff, and simply stop saving ourselves from anything, be it thought, boredom, energy, or the great nothing-is-happening itself.

11. If you think while doing this, OK: Simply note it.

12. There is no one to go back to. This is not *vipassana* meditation as most people understand it, and therefore we are not even interested in a "watcher" who will witness all of this stuff going on.

13. We couldn't care less.

14. We are going to simply sit here. You might say that we are "on strike" from our usual job of saving our self. In fact, form-anxiety work *uncovers* this often hidden, but omnipresent imperative in our lives, the omnipresent pressure to save ourselves.

15. The only thing you can pay attention to are the sensations in your body. But our attitude toward them will be: they don't matter. Having one type of sensation or another will not lead you closer to enlightenment. In fact, we don't care about enlightenment: We have no goal other than no longer saving ourselves.

16. We are going to simply do nothing for a while. We are going to give up all our strategies for "getting better," for "getting healthier," for "improving."

17. We are simply going to stop.

18. And even if these strategies continue, we are not even going to attempt to control or stop them.

19. Please practice this several times a week.

20. The Tibetan teacher Chögyam Trungpa calls this stage of relating to what I call the *what-is,* "nonmeditation"—and that is exactly what it is. When we talk about "being on strike," we are describing what it is like to sit in *nonmeditation,* which is not the same thing as either resisting meditation or seeking some specific goal or even observing all that goes on, since those activities only split the observing ego further into invisibility (though it does teach the ego to have more responsibility and equanimity . . .).

21. Form-anxiety reveals form-preciousness because in the state of *form-anxiety* we allow both the *impact* of the world and our egoic interaction with it to exist. Period. There is no strategy or manipulation . . . or if there is, that too lends its energy to the vividness of the world going about its business.

22. Every moment, every thing, every state is an equally potent object of meditation.

23. This very state, which is vast and small, particular and generalized, mundane and holy, in chains and completely free, is the state in which relating to the *continuity/density* becomes possible. And useful.

24. When everything is allowed to work together in this way, the nondual voyager will enter into the indeterminate world of suggestions, associations, glimpses, hums, smells and other sensory and ur-sensory experiences that he or she must then put together cogently.

    Entering the multi-dimensional world of voyaging

25. Further, we can even say that this indeterminacy exists in both space and time. Thus time and space for the nondual voyager are malleable, changeable, important and unimportant, in the sense of not being glamorous or part of the unhealed ego's need for entertainment.

26. Like the void that bubbles with the foam of existence and nonexistence, time and space both are in a constant state of metamorphosis and thus open to exploration, their relationship constantly reshaping itself and revealing facets once hidden.

27. We float—with open eyes—in the *space-time* mixture that is part of the basis of the *continuity/density* we have been so carefully cultivating, our consciousness altered by our ability to swim in this quantum sea.

28. It is worth mentioning that this is why this nondual approach does not rely on "intuition," or on the world telling you what to do. It does not despise knowledge but encourages it. It does not seek the monk but the householder, the engaged, busy person who takes the time to wander in ancient hills.

29. In addition, instead of emptying himself out, the voyager *includes all of his professional and life knowledge.*

30. In other words, you don't give up or throw away your psychological, medical, philosophical, educational, developmental, relational, poetic, scientific understandings. You don't throw away your family relationships or choose a lineage to which only the special can belong. You enter the world. It is sometimes a scary thing! Yet, you bring all of yourself to this event.

31. Let me quote from a Tibetan commentator on the *Kalacakratantra:*[*]

    The eyes of beginners—the very eyes that see pots, pillars, and so forth—see universal form in the sky, endowed with all aspects. That form is not ultimately existent because it is beyond atomic structure and because it is not produced through a process involving a "produced object" and a "producer." But it is still not nonexistent because it has the nature of the supreme and unchanging bliss and because (the shaman) sees it in the sky . . .

32. All the appearances voyagers see as they journey arise from the field, the same field that needs a soft (or *bucolic*) mind to apprehend it.[†]

---

[*] The Kalacakratantra is a Vajrayana Buddhist teaching that is based on time cycles or rhythm as a universal function. This rhythm extends to all domains: the rhythm of the planets and external universe as well as the internal rhythms of breathing, the circulation of blood, the pulsations of the nervous system and so on. Its application for personal liberation is considered an advanced teaching in the Tibetan tradition.

[†] In addition to what we have already mentioned, *bucolic mind* will be explored in greater depth later in the book.

33. There are no obstacles because none of the things the voyager sees are in opposition to other things.

34. The voyager sees paths, things to do, directions in which to go, things not to do, things to avoid. Yet, they all are part of this field in associative space-time, the pure poetry of the workings of the world.

35. The Tibetans call this "the play or *radiation* of awareness appearing in unclouded intensity."

36. For us, we might say that the voyager allows him or herself to exist in the synchronicity of the world, its vast, characterless spontaneity, and slowly, with trust in the healing ego, that narrative-making machinery of the psyche allows linear cause and effect to descend like a cloud on the universe's spontaneous field of dreams, making knowledge for someone from the emptiness of space.

37. Finally, I'll quote from a Tibetan story (as recounted in the book *Naked Seeing* by Christopher Hatchell*) about the yogi Gyerpunga, who, having glimpsed the state of utter unity, had become proud and obnoxious. He would have stayed that way had not another yogi, Tapihrista, appeared magically to Gyerpunga and taught him the true way. Tapihrista appears to Gyerpunga several times, the first time as a "precocious

---

* I am greatly indebted to Christopher Hatchell's book, *Naked Seeing: The Great Perfection, the Wheel of Time, and Visionary Buddhism in Renaissance Tibet*, Oxford University Press, 2014, a brilliantly written discourse on seeing as a path to enlightenment (among other things…). I have quoted liberally from his work and from his translation of seminal Tibetan works of the period.

wood-carrier boy." As quoted in *Naked Seeing*, in a famous exchange, Gyerpunga realized there was something unusual about the servant boy, and asked him with some hostility:

> *Your mind seems to have been affected by religious tenets . . . Who is your teacher? What experience have you had? What meditations do you perform? What is your burden? What is it that you are doing by acting as a wood carrier?*

> *The little boy replied:*

> *My teacher is ordinary appearance! I have had the experience of non-conceptuality. My meditation is all the appearance of the three realms. My burden is discursive thought. What I am doing is serving beings!*

38. That is ultimately what we are doing: serving beings. What we have in common with traditional shamanism is that we are members of the human tribe who have decided to specialize in this particular form of help for our fellow creatures.

39. The joy of this work—and what makes all the challenges worth the moments of confusion, limitation, frustration and even desperation—is that this is a good way to help. It opens the door to a different type of solace and healing, it walks by a different route and sometimes brings illumination to situations that were impenetrably dark. It uses darkness as a friend and finds hope in the field, along with berries for sustenance, fresh water to drink and the companionship of creation—which is who we are, and everywhere we look.

What World is This?

1. Traditional shamanism—as systemized and presented by the neo-shamanistic movement popular in the modern age—has divided the world into three (or more) separate domains: the lower world, the middle world, and the upper world, each with their own characteristics and usefulness in the art of healing.

2. Let me quote at length from a website[*] I found, which I felt was pretty clear and grounded in this traditional and neo-traditional approach:

   > *Within the shamanic cosmology, the world is divided into three levels: the upper, lower, and middle worlds. This is often symbolized by a world tree, with the roots, trunk, and branches corresponding to the lower, middle and upper worlds, respectively. This is the trinity of shamanism. Each level contains within it a certain vibrational quality that holds specific wisdom and healing that is accessible to the shaman by entering a non-ordinary or altered state of consciousness. The ability to enter the other reality is frequently achieved through the use of a drum, rattle, dancing, chanting, and medicine plants or mushrooms. The shaman travels through these three worlds to gather information and medicines that are specific for the person they are working with.*

---

[*] Organic Unity: http://www.organic-unity.com/top-menu/the-three-worlds-of-shamanism/

The lower world is commonly misperceived as being the place where evil spirits live, darkness pervades, and in general, not a good place. This is mainly due to our cultural conditioning of hell being "down there," and heaven being "up there." The lower world is in fact the place where many spirits of nature reside. It is a place where the essence of a plant, mineral, animal, mountain, lake, or any other aspect of nature can be connected and communed with. In this way, the lower world provides information into nature, and the invisible web of interconnections that it contains. It is often a place where one's power animals reside, as well as plant totems. The lower world could also be considered microcosmically to be our unconscious or subconscious self—those parts of our being which are constantly at play but yet we are unaware of.

The middle world is our reality as we know it. It is our day to day lives and residing place of our physical bodies and our normal waking consciousness. The middle world reality is full of trials and tribulations, tests and blessings—yet it is only one third of the tree of life. If we are not rooted in the wisdom of the lower world, our trunk will not be able to carry the nourishment that the branches need to reach full flowering. In order for our middle world reality to be understandable, a firm groundedness in the underworld is necessary—that is, entering a communion with the invisible dynamics of nature, the spiritual essences of the natural world. The middle world would be considered our ego, or conscious self.

> *The upper world is what some call the "heavens." This is the home of the star nations, our celestial or spirit guides, the angels and archetypes (12 astrological signs), and the planetary beings. Microcosmically, the upper world relates to our higher self, or super-consciousness that permeates across all time and space. The upper world is where we turn for spiritual guidance and wisdom that is of a higher vibrational quality than that of lower world wisdom. It is not better, just a different quality. The upper world reveals the depth of our true essential nature that will allow us to enter into the flowering of our purpose. It is our peak, our summit. It is here that we receive the guidance that will take us closer to being in harmony with the unity.*
>
> *Each world is an absolutely necessary part of our own being and the universe at large. Neither has teachings or healings that are better or worse than the other—they are just different.*

3. The approach from the perspective of nondual voyaging is somewhat different: Rather than dividing the world—even into useful parts—the nondual voyager sees only a single world with a multitude of *densities.*

    For the nondual voyager all dimensions are in the here and now.

4. This difference is not only theoretical or doctrinaire. By relating only to a *single world*, the *consciousness* of the voyager is changed. And further, the approach the voyager will take in helping others will be transformed as well.

5. We could say that the nondual voyager has given up even the hope of an escape from

the *here-is* and simultaneously learned that this *here-is* is infinite by every measure. In other words, every conceivable dimension is already and actually here.

6. Simply relating to the three worlds as if they were somehow separate from this here-and-now does not change the consciousness of the voyager because the voyager's identity remains separate from the rest of the world. In other words, subject and object, as a paradigm for understanding the world and the self, remains untouched.

7. The acceptance of the truth that this is a single world and that all domains are present as *densities*, as features of the *continuity* (whether more or less vivid), changes the voyager's perspective as to themselves and the world they live in. In a sense, this acceptance that "there is nowhere else to go," is a sort of revelation that enables the voyager to relate to the world—and to themselves—as part of the *continuity/density*. This has the effect of allowing the voyager to see other people—themselves *densities* in the *continuity*—in a different light as well.

   > The voyager also knows that problems sometimes live in *densities* other than the ones that are most prominent.
   >
   > Voyaging, which is nonlinear and because of this, open to synchronicity, brilliant associations and dumb luck, can properly discern through a panoramic perspective.

8. We might say that every person who walks into the voyager's practice room is someone who is intrinsically whole but perhaps confused or unconscious as to which *density* their ego is concentrating on, making some views more "real" than other views that might afford more healing and wholeness.

9. Problems with the *choices* we make (or that were made for us at some point in the past), and which cause us to focus our attention

on thoughts, feelings and desires that did not serve us, can show up as physical, mental, emotional or spiritual dissonances.

10. Because of the nature of space and time as it relates to the work of the nondual voyager, these problems can be in the personal past, present or future. A single world contains all times, past, present and future, and so time in the voyager's *milieu* is part of the voyager's playground.

11. This is not to say that discerning all of this will heal all ailments. That is not the only purpose or aim of the nondual voyager.

12. Instead, one internal purpose of the nondual voyager should really be the answer to this question: *How do I, with the limitations I have, with the less-than-perfect understanding I am capable of, with the wounded parts of my body that might always afflict me, live a life of wholeness, pleasure and service?*

13. Wanting this for themselves, solving this conundrum for themselves, the voyager automatically wants this for all other beings. And that is how it should be. Healing the voyager's own self heals others and healing others heals the voyager. It is always—and must be—a two-way street.

14. The starting point of a *single world with an infinite number of densities* is the beginning of forming a relationship—first within the healer themselves—that can bring forth this level of healing, along with any relative-level healing we are capable of initiating or

supporting, which, of course, continues to be important.

15. The perspective of "one world" can challenge the voyager's personal level of realization.

16. It does that because to have deeply accepted living in a single, unitive world—in one place at one time, with no hope of there being a heaven or hell, afterlife or other form of spiritual escape *(whether there are such places or not!)*—the voyager must have found a way to commit to a form of spiritual work that brings the foreground of the personal and the background of the transcendent or impersonal self into complete relationship, to bring everything in this *one-thought-moment* or "one moment of time that continues forever."

17. In other words, the nondual voyager is working from the assumption, foundation, and (hopefully) the experience of the mutual and inevitable co-arising of self and other, nirvana and samsara, the absolute and the relative, sickness and health.

18. The nondual voyager must have come to the understanding that *both parts of any pair of polar opposites are useful to a life dedicated to wholeness.*

19. To say it another way, they have come to understand that failure has value, as does suffering, as does any so-called negative condition, while *at the same time,* they choose to heal these conditions so that the individual can live a life as free as possible of these obstructions.

20. We have to know who the allies truly are and be ready to meet them the way Buddha had tea with Mara, the master of illusion and disappointment.

21. For Buddha, there were not two worlds: the world of Buddha and the world of Mara. Though Buddha's attendant Ananda (which means *bliss*) tried to keep Mara separate and at bay, Buddha overruled him and invited Mara to a friendly conversation.

22. To do this, we must begin to break the chains of a specific type of limitation, namely, to no longer be limited by the narrow, myopic-specific vision that the unhealed ego has of our life and destiny.

23. We must begin to see that the ego, rather than being an actual thing, is simply a context or experience much like any other, to be no more exclusively believed in than any other experience.

> And yet, the ego *is* real. It is just as it is. The path of the nondual voyager asks us to not disrespect the ego—even if it is a temporary manifestation—but instead heal it, so it can aid us and be our best part instead of our constant adversary.

24. We must begin to see that the context of the self is larger than the small focal area the ego's sight is concentrated on.

25. This must be the voyager's authentic, personal experience and the area of the voyager's dedicated, ongoing exploration.

A Single World

1. The acceptance of a single world follows naturally as we let go of every back door and resistance to being here. It comes into our understanding as we are able, through our psychological healing and insight, to reduce our fear of being alive physically, emotionally, mentally and psychically.

2. Until we are able to do that, we might reach out to "other worlds" as a way of defending ourselves from being in this one, with its tragedies and joys, suffering and healing.

3. The important decision to be fully *here* and not use the thought or concept of "other worlds" to escape the difficulties of the here and now does not preclude the existence of other dimensions, worlds and subtle states of consciousness that the human mind, body and spirit are capable of experiencing.

4. But when these subtle realms are not encountered from a defensive position or in order to offer the possibility of escape from this physical life, we have the opportunity of understanding them from a different and much more creative vantage point: as facets of a single world that extends infinitely in all directions.

5. The here-and-now does not *contain* these different realms and dimensions: it is *made* of them.

6. This allows us to partake of them, engage with them and even use them in a way that is not possible when their very existence is

part of a strategic attempt to save the self from the uncertainties of this life.

7. All possible dimensions and worlds are integral to this one. There is no wholeness possible without the radical acceptance of the here and now as the totality of our life.

8. Even if we think that at the point of death we simply disappear forever, we must risk that possibility in favor of this being our only life.

9. This emotional and psychological *collapse into a location,* is like the collapse of the wave function in physics:

    A collapse of the wave function is what happens when any physical state—after being observed by measurement—changes from one of superposition (which is to say a complex of possible states, locations and momentums) to a single location, a single place and a single manifestation.

10. Probability collapses into specificity, so to speak. Now there is a "here" to which our own "here" can relate. There is now a single "here."

11. We could even say that this reality becomes (though it always was so…) actualized (which is to say filled with *densities*) and continuous (which is to say a *continuity*).

12. The here-and-now—which is both the outer and inner world—is now ready to reveal itself *to itself,* to unfold within a consciousness that has become the proper instrument to perceive it.

13. It is useful for us to know this concept in physics because we can apply it to our consciousness. In other words, we can use this metaphor to help us understand how our consciousness can change.

14. A change in consciousness is one definition of what learning is.

15. This does not mean that this sort of learning nullifies confusion or any other ambiguous state. This here-and-now is not a cage or a prison. Instead, because it allows everything in, it actually allows those prior states to become a conscious part of wholeness. This sort of learning is cumulative and layered; it does not discard earlier information because it has been supplanted by a new and perhaps bigger view. Instead, in this new context, states such as confusion, ambiguity, boredom, failure and mistakes take on new meaning and depth.

16. Prior to this, those states were in *opposition to what we thought wholeness was, what awakening was, or what a healed person actually is.* Now, in this integrative approach, we can see freshly the usefulness of all the earlier states.

17. Learning, in this case, is a form of enlarging our consciousness to contain more of the world as it actually is.

18. Whether it occurs as a flash of insight or bit by bit, as in a new relationship with practice, is irrelevant. This moment of *locating* changes our consciousness.

19. To restate this specifically about the spiritual journey: every learning along the spiritual path is brought about by the transformation of miasmatic understanding into one of specificity, clarity and completeness, *even if this new arrangement or completeness contains or includes confusion, ambiguity and other uncertain elements.* All of the elements of the human periodic table are present . . . and needed.

20. The point is: things begin to be what they are with fewer and fewer overlays of old historical and neurotic thinking. This is a big deal and is mostly met with resistance, confusion, boredom, a sense of inadequacy, and outright hostility for many of us much of the time.

21. Paths that emphasize a sudden revelatory moment miss the point. Although a revelation may show us the mountain top illuminated in a flash of lightening for a moment, the only way this understanding or this flash—if it comes—can be stabilized over time is with a relationship with practice, in our case, the practice of self-knowledge.

    IYI:
    The ego naturally resists change and prefers homeostasis. This has a downside for its other ambition, which is to grow. We must also remember that both of these egoic ambitions, homeostasis and growth, when working together, are responsible for what we call "healing."

22. Eventually a deeper understanding emerges, the fact that enlightenment *is* practice, rather than practice *bringing* enlightenment. Awakening is the surrender to practice.

23. All of this is to say that the nondual voyager must be involved with practice forever. There is no graduation from this school of learning reality since reality is the name we give to the *relationship* between an observing

ego and the treasure chest of possibilities
that make up the external world.

The Turn

1. One of my practices is *gazing* into various transparent and semi-transparent materials: glass, water, crystal balls and so on.

    Tibetan Bon shamans gazed (variously) into darkness, smoke, water, and bright, empty skies.

2. These elements or devices hold no intrinsic magic in and of themselves—outside of the fundamental magic of the fact that the material world even exists!

3. Instead, for me, they are machines that aid me in the *turn* I must make to enter into this new relationship with my own consciousness and thus, into a new relationship with that part of reality called "the world."

4. This *turn* is not only specific and unique to each shaman but also understandable and comprehensible to each shaman who has done their own *turn*—whether it is similar to their own *turn* or not. A voyager can spot another voyager.

5. In other words, just as in the *turn* in Impersonal Movement*—which Arlene Shulman reminded me is a precursor to this one—we know when it is authentic or not, even if there are a multitude of *turns* possible.

6. The *turn* is internally proprioceptive and might be experienced by the voyager through a multitude of means: a change in temperature or color, or size or dimension,

    What the *turn* is and how to recognize it

---

* For more a more extensive description of Impersonal Movement, please see the section called *Additional Exercises for the Nondual Voyager* later in this book.

a falling back within oneself, a leaving of the body or a gentle movement of the energy body forward or back. For many people, it is something they have learned to do unconsciously over a long period of time without paying attention to this rather amazing reconfiguration of the energy system of the physical body.

7. It becomes the job of the voyager to make this *turn* conscious and replicable.

8. For some people, this *turn* might involve just consciousness alone or might also include touching various objects to bring about this *turn:* stone, a twig, a crystal, a piece of metal, in short, *anything that is helpful.**

9. Again, for some people, these kinesthetic/proprioceptive feelings might not even be registered as sensations in the body, or sensations in internal body organs, tendons, muscles and so on. Instead, they may take place *entirely in the mental body image,* that sense we keep in our minds—in a mostly unconscious way—of our body in space, a sort of phenomenological body.

10. Interestingly enough, the more we work to become sensitive to this internal body image, its imaginal pressures, torques, waves and other sensitivities, the more we arrive at

---

* From the point of view of the nondual voyager, objects only have power or usefulness to the extent that they remind the voyager of the truth of a unity that is a single thing, which simultaneously has different parts. For some it might be a beautiful *objet d'art*. For others, a pebble or a bottle cap might do. This is a touching and rather moving understanding and part of the awakening process itself. Yet, it is an equally complex topic that will take patience for the voyager to understand and inhabit. I will go into more about this later in the chapter called *The Gift: Making Magic Manifest.*

the plain, unadorned sensory apprehension of our actual, physical body, the body with "nowhere to go." This type of body is the perfect vehicle for healing and the exploration of the cosmos itself.

"Nowhere to go" is another way of talking about the personal self in a *single world*. It is a powerful and freeing state to live in but it takes disappointment and disillusionment for the ego to get there.

11. This is the body that is no longer confused by its history or its historical woundings, not because they have all magically disappeared but, exactly opposite to that fantasy, because they have all been *located*.

12. When things are located, they are no longer miasmatic, which is to say, no longer atmospheric and invisible and therefore penetrating and unconsciously acted out. Located, they have become "substance," which can be noticed, used, avoided, understood, ignored and ultimately accepted as part of the totality of one's being.

Everything is "on the table."

13. Please look at *The Silent Body* (included a little further on in this book), as a guide to the apprehension and inhabitation of this fundamental, physical state, a state that is filled with grace directly because of its direct, unadorned plainness.

14. This completely physicalized, located body becomes the center of the vast space we call the here-and-now or *what-is*. It is through this vehicle that we can enter into a new relationship with the universe, the universe that contains yesterday, tomorrow, right now and all the dimensions and even beings who inhabit those realms.

15. This new level of connection to our physical body (and the plainness that is its hallmark)

opens additional doors for the nondual voyager as he or she dares to sit in this single world—the single world that contains this temporary physical mass (our body)—and experience the infinite openings that occur when we are simply who we are. More about this later.

Images

1. Because the nondual voyager may use imagery in their work—whether this imagery is visual, auditory, tactile or conceptual—in order to both learn and see the path forward, I'd like to talk about the nondual perspective on this type of imagery.

2. Let me quote from a Wikipedia article on mental imagery:

    A mental image or mental picture is the representation in a person's mind of the physical world outside of that person. It is an experience that, on most occasions, significantly resembles the experience of perceiving some object, event, or scene, but occurs when the relevant object, event, or scene is not actually present to the senses. There are sometimes episodes, particularly on falling asleep (hypnogogic imagery) and waking up (hypnopompic), when the mental imagery, being of a rapid, phantasmagoric and involuntary character, defies perception, presenting a kaleidoscopic field, in which no distinct object can be discerned.[*]

3. One of the times or places in which most humans engage in mental imagery is in the space between waking and sleeping, or in reverse, between sleeping and waking up. This type of hypnogogic imagery (which I use to refer to both pre-sleep *hypnogogic* and post-sleep *hypnopompic* imagery) often has

---

[*] https://en.wikipedia.org/wiki/Mental_image

an a-logical, a-causal, hallucinatory quality to it.

4. The traditional way hypnogogic imagery is explained falls into two main camps: those who think it is built around our thinking process, made from the imagery and objects we have seen or heard, touched or smelled during the day, and those who think it is purely made out of images that spring directly from the nervous system and have little or nothing to do with actual events but are used by the brain to encode and decode information. In other words, we are just seeing the nervous system's mechanisms couched in a narrative or visual form.

5. The nondual voyager's view on this is different, of course. From this point of view, the nervous system *is* the outside world since we only see that which our nervous system is capable of perceiving.

> The nondual view

6. We could say that our nervous system participates in the creation of what we see and that there is no purely objective (read: separate) "there" there, without the coloration or *information* the nervous system itself provides.

7. Likewise, this point of view suggests that there is no purely subjective "here" as well, since what we take for our subject is a participatory quality co-created by a seemingly outer "over there"—and the seemingly inner "over here."

8. Again, to put it another way, so-called "inner" and so-called "outer" are co-arising phenomena, nondual phenomena if you

will; they need each other to exist at all. What we take for "there" is a combination of "here" and "there," while what we take for "here" is again the same combination, subjective and objective, foreground and background nested together, looked at from different points of view.

9. To give an example: If we say *the automobile designed the highway*, this might be seen as an illogical thought: the roads were designed *for* automobiles. But actually, it *is a* two-way street: *the car, with its rubber tires, powerful engine, agile suspension and enclosed cabin "calls out for a road" that is smooth, resilient, and mostly flat, with lanes, negotiable curves and so on.* Thus the car, instead of being a passive partner, has design input into the road engineer's design . . . and vice versa.

10. So when we see a scene or person or object, we are seeing the nervous system as well as what stimulated the nervous system.

11. But, in addition, the nondual view also recognizes that the outside world *is* the nervous system.

12. In other words, the nervous system was made and organized, shaped and structured by the outside world and its chemical realities, atomic and structural necessities, its gravity and movements and so on. So "our" nervous system is "the world's" nervous system from a non-personal or impersonal point of view. Sentient beings are the sensorium of the world since it decided, in a sense, to have one.

13. If we apply these perspectives to our hypnagogic or hypnopompic imagery, we can only say that it *is* our nervous system—which includes of course, the images and contact this nervous system had with the world *and* the "out-gassing" of this nervous system's energy at the same time. The two are not different but mingled.

14. What is revealed by our nervous system then, is ourselves, this self that is *continuous* with inside and outside. It is a river that flows in two directions at once.

15. Since *continuity/density* is our benchmark for what reality is, our hypnogogic imagery is the expression or manifestation of the indivisible continuity between self and other, external and internal, and even material and non-material.

16. Our imagery, from this point of view, is our direct contact with the totality of being.

17. And though the personal self will be skillfully brought back into the picture, this imagery is not owned by the personal self, is not a product of the personal self alone, and, because of that, is not simply an image of some purely—or only—psychological process within the voyager.

18. This imagery spans the demarcation line our personal ego thinks is a real place of true separateness rather than a convenience.

19. For the untrained layman, hypnogogic imagery has only the presentation of *a kaleidoscopic field in which no distinct object can*

be discerned (which is to imply that while it is a beautiful display, it is essentially meaningless), while for the trained nondual voyager it has both the information of the overall pattern *and* the information of the simultaneously-arising specifics: it contains oneness *and* difference—and therefore a new level of insight.

20. The *turn* I spoke about before is the nondual voyager's way of getting to the hypnogogic state while still completely awake.

    > Stepping into knowing

21. I might add here that even using the term *hypnogogic* might be misleading: this *turn* brings us to a state that is not one of sleepiness or trance. In a way we can say it brings us *out* of trance *into* contact with what reality is like when it is not covered in unconscious assumptions and directed by an unexplored ego.

    > Are we in the "now" then? Hard to say, since the here-and-now extends through the past and future in this single world.

22. When we wake up or when we drop slightly into sleep, many of our so-called higher functions of discernment—which can also be read as egoic hyper-foci—fall away and we are presented with a representation of the world that has not yet been organized by memory, comparison, habit or a prior list of feelings.

23. What happens next is that we enter into a sort of participatory or creative process that molds these images into something previously known. Thus, we *identify* these images and blend them into a narrative that has historical meaning for us. Most of this—unless we are trained—goes on unconsciously.

24. If we were Freudians, we might say that the voyager's view sees primary process, all introjections, conscious states and unconscious states (with the proviso that for a nondual explorer, even unconscious states can be experienced in their original form).

25. If we were Jungians, we would add our connection to all archetypical realms. And if we went beyond Jung's *anthropocentric* idea of archetypes, we could see these realms as *bleed-through* or inklings of some of the underlying forces that made human beings the way they are. This is to say, not as projections of the human mind but as *"prior instruction sets" that guided the creation of the human mind itself.*

26. All of this allows us to have a "bigger set" through which to listen, understanding that our client is not pointing us to "reality," but rather the content of reality their "narrator of the moment" wants us to hear and see—while the narrator remains invisible.

    The voyager listens with *bucolic mind*, a mind at ease. The voyager is always strolling and meandering through the neighborhood.

27. In this new way, we hear the content *and* the presence of the narrator who is now visible. Both the subjective and objective poles become visible simultaneously. In other words, we can see the presence of the narrator within the meta-narrative of the totality of that person's being. We hear the tale of both the trees *and* the forest at the same time.

28. Once we are aware of the existence of the narrator, we can see the narrator *as part of the story*, a character in the story itself.

29. The nondual voyager of course, is attempting to live this way as well as *heal others* in this manner.

30. In doing this, the nondual voyager sees no difference between inner and outer but, for that moment of voyaging, is electrified by the single world that manifests constantly as himself (or the inner world) and the outer world. There is an atmosphere of *continuity/density* between the voyager and the one he or she is working with—and yet no merging of identities; separateness and oneness are both part of the totality.

31. The voyager becomes a bridge, but a bridge to nowhere, since there really is no chasm or river to cross.

32. "Ordinary" reality is consensual reality, the statistical norm, a single moment in the bell-curve of possible human experience.

33. The nondual voyager consciously decides to step out of that consensus *at will,* and in doing that, resides in a truth-telling place where language, approach, coloration and tone might be different from the way insight is expressed in the consensually-oriented worldview.

34. The *turn* can be taught or, rather, it can be learned. But it is not learned through either rote or explanatory teaching. It can only be learned by contact with another nondual voyager, both in a specific learning situation and with contact with the voyager-teacher's ordinary, quotidian world.

35. How the master voyager "eats his or her breakfast," to emulate an old kabbalistic tale, is as important as any erudite forays into galactic spheres.

36. The true learning, the learning that stays, comes from the apprentice voyager's internal dynamo, which churns out the message, again and again, *go there*. It is a message of encouragement.

37. I have included below the entirety of "The Silent Body."

38. This piece is made to be worked with on a detailed basis by the voyager. It is a direct transmission of the experience of the body in its awakening state, that state through which the constancy of the continuity between the inner and outer world is seen.

The Silent Body

1. The silent body is without thought, beneath story and beyond conceptualization. Because it is these things, it is in the province of the Great Mother, Shakti.

2. The Great Mother Shakti, who is not a person, who is not an object, who is not separate from us in any way, can only appear when the body is no longer a ghost.

3. The body is a ghost when it narrates life to feel alive instead of living it.

4. To achieve the silent body, the body must return to truth and leave—at least for a while—symbolic speech.

5. Symbolic speech arises when the bodymind—which is limited in time to Now—tries to experience a Now as if this now could be somewhere, somewhen else than where it is now, someplace pristine that does not include its totality.

6. Symbolic speech arises when we listen to the echo instead of the sound.

7. Symbolic speech arises when the mind—which is the thinking part of the body—makes the body its psychological shadow and tells the story it believes is true instead of the one that is actual.

8. It then enters "story" and is in the realm of the representational, the symbol for the thing instead of the thing.

9. On the road to the silent body, we must encounter the body-as-corpse, the body that is all in history, since the true Now has not been found or experienced.

10. Seeing that the body is in history is part of seeing the body in the actual Now.

11. We fear letting the body return to the silence of non-symbolic speech, the speech of no sound, no place but here, no strategy but our actions in the moment. Our mind believes that aliveness must be made in its own image. The fear is that by allowing the body to return to silence, we will lose who we are. In other words, thinking we are the body in some narrow image of Now, some idea of the Now, any change threatens our existence, any relaxing brings us the fear that we will disappear.

12. Our mind in its present state has a small identity. We have an innate psychic part of our minds that fears any change, whether for good or ill, that believes it needs to make the world over in its own image, within its own imagination, in order to survive.

13. When the world changes—for change it must—this unhealed ego, this troublesome part that will eventually become our friend, fears for its life.

14. So, as infant and child, young adult, adult and elder, if we are unknown to ourselves, we work to keep life small and—though professing the love of growth and change—work for its enemies instead.

15. Thus the movement into the *first* stage of oneness—when we experience the pure unity of all things without the later addition of *difference*—is difficult.

16. This first experience is the experience in which all landmarks disappear, the place beyond, and before, speech, the stage before we have returned to the marketplace, once more in deep conversation with life-as-it-is on the ground.

17. We fear to go into this silence because it feels like—and is—a kind of death. It is a numberless place, and it is the first place we must inhabit on the way to the body's return to its home as the Abode of the Mother, the Hum of Shakti, which forms around itself the entire material universe, with its singleness of differences, its unity of opposites, its illuminating darkness.

18. Where is the body-as-corpse? This is not a mental exercise, some arcane practice that exists to teach us something. It is simply the truth. It is right here if we know how to look.

19. When we touch the tip of our finger to a cold piece of metal, we experience an analog of reality: we feel the coldness in the finger, though in actuality, what the finger "feels" is simply the activation and firing of a sequence of nerves. These nerves, already-in-history, that is, in the past, in reaction to what already-is, send a message to the brain, which interprets this feeling into already-known memories of cold and heat, metal and glass, and sends this impulse down to the fingertip via other nerves.

20. When this is realized, the body is seen clearly as a mechanism, an elaborate, wonderful mechanism, but a mechanism nonetheless.

21. A machine that pretends to be alive is still pretending. But a machine that knows itself to be a machine is placed squarely in the real Now, beyond the unhealed mind's hemmed-in version of what aliveness is.

22. It is resurrected, restored, removed from illusion. It is not sad about this. Any tears that fall are tears of joy because the truth brings a kind of rain that comforts all beings.

23. In searching for awakening, we are not looking for a picture of life, but life itself, as it is. In other words, before a return to the body-as-life can be made, the body must recede from its powerful position to the background, as it were, so that another, more potent movement can come to the fore. So that we can see that this Now we hope so deeply for contains everything and everywhen. History, it turns out, is in the Now as well.

24. This movement allows us to see the body as a wonderful lump of clay.

25. We cannot enter this state until we have become thoroughly familiar with our historical defenses, which always seek to dissociate us from our pain.

26. Our unhealed sense of self wants to *be somebody*. But this "somebody" is an unconscious bulwark against the sea of

reality. It is a construction of defenses and is not yet a real girl or a real boy.

27. The silent body, the true body of Christ before the resurrection, is not arrived at through the need for a defense, but because of the fearless stance of the warrior, who is willing to go into nothingness in pursuit of God.

28. Why "the body of Christ before the resurrection?" Because Christ's power lay in his being who he was for no other reason than being who he was, which was his reason for being. It should be the same for us.

29. How do we change? We must let go of the past. To "let go" of the past means we must be willing to make enormous effort to work this history through, to have the support to work it through, as well.

30. Letting go of the past does not mean the past no longer exists, but now it exists *as the past* and not as an echo we believe is still sounding. The past, residing in the room of our present self, is part of who we are, part of our totality but not its central part.

31. Everything becomes itself, something it always was.

32. When seen through this process, the body-as-corpse is a wonderful, freeing thing. Looking through these dead eyes at the world, we see for the first time how the truly dead masquerades as life while the dead we have found is life-in-action, each thing being itself, separate and connected to

every other thing, no longer covered over in expectation, denial and hope.

33. We see around us the tragedy of life and its immediate, constant scintillation. We see the questing people, desperate for the Real, looking the other way.

34. The path to the silent body is the same as any of the paths to God: we must learn about ourselves; we must quiet the mind; we must act with kindness toward the self.

35. The thing that is new here is the idea that we are not—by doing all of this—moving toward some spiritually athletic vision of an "alive body."

36. Instead, we are looking for the body to get quieter and quieter, until, no longer speaking to us in its various tongues, the mechanism behind its façade of realness appears and our consciousness begins to see that we are the body, but that this body, in this form of the real, extends in all directions, humble and kind, limited and yet a temporary repository for the waves of this eternal world. This realization makes all the difference.

37. The bones are silent: remember this.

38. The muscles and tendons are silent: remember this.

39. The lungs fill and deflate. They are nothing but what they are.

40. The deeper we sink into things, the happier we are, being one with our true nature.

41. It is paradoxical: to be alive, let the body die. The dead body, the silent body, is freely alive as the body itself.

42. When we overeat, we are not in the silent body. Overeating, and every other indulgence, including the pursuit of pleasure, is a futile attempt to "stay alive."

43. The path toward the silent body at that moment is awareness and immediate self-acceptance and forgiveness, no matter what the transgression.

44. When we cannot forgive ourselves for our misconduct and limited self, we are in the conceptual body, the imaginal body, which is actually separate from who we are, a sort of idealization of what or who we think we are or should be. When we are in those states, we are not in the silent body.

45. The silent body makes love because that is its nature: to join flesh to flesh; the silent body sings because it itself is song.

46. Walking along the bay in Truro, I picture men and women with salt traps making salt from sea water almost two hundred years ago.

47. This same type of salt, now sold as gourmet salt called *fleur de sel*, is what everyone commonly used to salt their food until sodium chloride mines were discovered in France in the early nineteenth century.

48. Unlike *fleur de sel*, which is from sea water, sodium chloride is relatively pure. *Fleur de sel* has ten or twenty trace minerals, which

have been lost in the translation to mined table salt. Boron, molybdenum, arsenic, copper, lithium, the list goes on.

49. The silent body loves the complexity of mineral rhythms. It loves the curves of arms swaying, or pelvis swaying and mouth opening and closing. It loves difference and abhors simplification, whether in medicine, politics, art, or relationship. Fascism is simple. Democracy is messy and complex. Manufactured bread turns to sugar quickly. Hand-made, whole grain bread develops slowly in the body, reducing to vitamins, minerals and the stuff of life.

50. The silent body loves nuance and subtlety. It lives in the constant life that takes place at the crossroads between things, the bazaars at the outskirts of town, the meeting places where stories are swapped.

51. The silent body, the body that is dead to symbolic speech, can do this. It is the proper vehicle for human life.

52. The silent body learns by engaging the world and its practices. It does not learn to engage, but engages and then learns. It is not in charge of its curriculum except to show up. That is its nature.

53. To the best of its ability—since it is a limited thing—the silent body, and all of its parts, wants to do its job of living. The lungs want to breathe and transfer oxygen and carbon dioxide. The ovaries want to make eggs and the prostate, fluid. The eyes want to flutter, keep moist, and see.

54. The body also wants to fall apart, because, as it is temporary, it wants to do that too. The silent body is the body in life and death.

55. The body itself should not ultimately be a repository for all of our psychological conflicts. That is using the body as an illness.

56. It is the keeper of psychological mysteries only so far as they have not been worked through. As they are worked through, they either leave altogether, or remain—non-symbolically, as crease or cut, bend or break, in the body proper.

57. Leaving psychology and symbolic speech behind, the body is free and then frees the mind, which is holy too.

58. Not talkative, not listening, not alive, not dead, we begin to see in the presence this silence has that it is the perfect screen for the manifestation of the Great Mother.

59. As our eyes grow dead, they open and see that all forms appear because of the Great Mother's existence. We are not filled with life, we do not contain life, but are life.

60. If we simply contained life, then upon the death of the physical body, we would lose our life forever. But dying first, we have the chance of seeing that our most essential self is the Great Mother herself. Our bodies are our Great Speech, the life we lead, Her spoken tongue.

61. No eyes, no ears, no mouth, no tongue: Giving up the pursuit of life, life comes to us. Knowing our body is a simulacrum, we enjoy its flight into the unknown.

62. Then when we speak, no dust comes out of our mouths, no moth wings, no sand. We speak with the tongues of angels then, which is to say, completely human, held as we are, in the fine forms of the Mother's earth.

An Excursion into Quality

1. This chapter can be helpful in getting a bodily sense of what *quality* is. *Quality* is the term we give to the illumination that arises as we become capable of holding *continuity/density* as a single thing. It is that simultaneity that makes each *density* glow with the illuminating aspect of the physical location of the *continuity*.

2. As we become practiced at living in *quality*, "foreground" and "background" no longer capture the sense that everything—all created things, including our own body, mind, and spirit—come forward into the same plane. The world from this point of view of equality is filled with the sense of fertility that the voyager comes to know well.

   Again, when everything is "on the table," everything is equally important. This is a *horizontal* vision rather than a vertical one. This is another road to *bucolic mind* since we are open to everything, not knowing which of these *features* of reality are important.

3. At the same time, this abundance is not overwhelming. It is organized by the various hues and tones of vividness—or *density*—which make up the particulars of the *continuity*. Our nervous system is not overwhelmed but actually relaxed, as all things are connected and supportive of everything else.

4. As our consciousness is held in this way, whatever is needed comes to mind, whether big or small, vivid or faint.

5. Then the conceptual and technical aspects of *features* and *featurelessness*, along with *bucolic mind* and *imagery*, come into play as the foundations we can count on in this dance with *quality* we make as we voyage.

6. This next section is meant to capture a bit of that state of wisdom and scintillation by the co-arising of *continuity* and *density*.

The Difference Quality Makes

1. Imagine for a moment you are on the deck of a ship as it sails northward, out of the harbor you call home, into uncharted waters.

   You are on the deck alone and you're quiet, yet excited and happy: you have left one section of your life and are entering another. It is beginning to get cold, just cold enough that you can feel fall entering the world, and the fall entering reminds you that winter will enter soon too. You are not afraid. You feel cozy and pull your light jacket around you and gaze out toward the reddening sun. The rest of the journey will be made in the night.

2. Reading this passage, you might feel something. What is it you feel? Though it doesn't relate to your life on a factual basis, metaphorically, it might: the story of starting a new journey on a ship and how your journeys might coincide in some ways. Yet, the moment that you read it, before you consider it, before you actually *think* about it, you have a sense, a feeling in your body, a broadness in your mind. Stop and see if this is true.

3. Whatever this "thing" is that makes you feel this way, this is what we are after, and it can be found in every aspect of your life, in everything that moves or does not move on the earth, in the laws that govern the heavens, in all of life and death.

4. All spiritual systems are attempts at getting to this notion of *quality*. All art that is great

art must have this as an ingredient. All political systems—no matter how distorted they may have become—are trying to find this. All of these endeavors are trying to "get to that thing" that feels real, whole, authentic, fair, alive and human.

5. Artists have painted mountains and houses forever. Why? What are they trying to depict? Certainly not mountains and houses but rather the *quality* they evoke. And evoke not just in the human heart, but as a universal constant. Cézanne attempted it by looking at light; Constable and Turner by looking at color and form; Rembrandt's etching of street scenes attempted it in yet other ways.

6. This *quality* is the union of the specific—houses, windows, clouds, trees, light and air—combined in such a way that they not only *point* to something universal and beyond the individual pieces, but the universal is *enshrined* in the relationship of the parts themselves.

7. The parts *are* the light and are also *illuminated* by the light. What is left is beyond words, a pervading silence we can—as voyagers—bring back to the world of words.

8. Here is a passage from Marcel Proust whose book *In Search of Lost Time* is entirely about this almost invisible thing we are calling *quality* and how all of life revolves around it. In this brief passage, Proust is describing, in great detail, the many things that happen to him as he falls asleep and awakes.

Childhood sleep, adult sleep, future sleep, all sleep, sway and mix in this telling:

> *Perhaps the immobility of the things around us is imposed on them by our certainty that they are themselves and not anything else, by the immobility of our mind confronting them. However that may be, when I woke thus, my mind restlessly attempting, without success, to discover where I was, everything revolved around me in the darkness, things, countries, years. My body, too benumbed to move, would try to locate, according to the form of its fatigues, the position of its limbs so as to deduce from this the direction of the wall, the placement of the furniture, so as to reconstruct and name the dwelling in which it found itself. Its memory, the memory of its ribs, its knees, its shoulders, offered in succession several of the rooms where it had slept, while around it the invisible walls, changing place according to the shape of the imagined room, spun through the shadows.*

9. Try reading this passage as a nondual voyager, watching and participating in the revolving, changing world.

10. Here are two short exercises for sensing *quality*. Please note how they use the *specific* to arrive at the unitive state:

Quality Meditation

1. Begin to think about some friendships you have. Pick good ones, people you like being with.

2. Feel the feeling they give you.

3. Now go on to another. Perhaps you can think of two or three.

4. Now: drop all the circumstances and particulars. Concentrate on the *feeling* these friendships give you <u>without</u> names, faces, or the people themselves.

5. What is left is a sort of "golden glow." That is my word, but you may have another: Spaciousness. Openness. Silence.

6. Just be with that "glow" (use your own word . . .) and let it fill you. It is beyond a personal feeling. It is not about "you" or anyone else. We could call this *quality*.

Beautiful Creatures

1. Picture a physical object that you have on you now or that you own. Something specific. Something you find beautiful. Maybe it's a watch or a scarf or a vase. But it is something real.

2. I'll use the image of a watch I own.

3. Look at the watch (or your own object).

4. It is beautiful, and it gives you a sensation when you look at it or think about it.

5. That sensation lingers even when you stop thinking about the specific object, when you've put it back in the drawer, so to speak.

6. This sensation is beyond the ingredients that make up the watch. It's not the gold case. It's not the crystal or the carefully painted watch dial.

7. It's not the leather band.

8. None of the characteristics of the watch or scarf can account for this sensation you get when you allow the whole object to affect you. In fact, you could do this with a number of objects and come to the *same exact sensation* . . . this sensation that is left after you drop all the specifics, the particular characteristics of the objects you have chosen.

9. So this sensation does not reside in any of the materials, though the arrangement of these materials creates a sense of beauty that is beyond the thing itself. This sensation has nothing to do with your *personal feeling* about the watch or scarf.

10. If you look carefully, you'll see that this sensation doesn't even exactly reside in you or the object. You are feeling it in *your* body, but it doesn't really belong to you or the object.

11. It belongs to no one. Nothing can capture it.

12. Be with all of that.

Additional Exercises for the Nondual Voyager

A note: since this is an advanced text, it presupposes that many readers of this material will have studied Impersonal Movement 1 and 2 with a qualified teacher. We could say that Impersonal Movement is one of the most important physical practices for the Nondual Voyager since it is the physical expression of many of the concepts in this book. Please see the information at the end of this book, which describes how to study this vital discipline.

IM, as we call it, is a series of steps and additions, movements really, that were created in response to various states of consciousness rather than being prescribed positions or movements. They are designed to give the practitioner a body-sense of the awakening self. The practice combines experiences associated with the absolute and with the personal self in a way that allows the student to enter into what we would call the "truly nondual." This understanding of the nondual state combines the personal in a special form we call "the personal-with-no-history" with an experience of the absolute. Only both together can help the student of spirituality enter into the totality of their being, that space in which no part of them is rejected but instead, returns to wholeness and to its intrinsic light.

For those readers who have studied IM, my hope is that the following material will allow them to enter into IM in a new way and that IM will help bring them to the consciousness of the voyager in a powerful way.

For those who have not studied Impersonal Movement 1 and 2, I encourage you to pursue learning this important part of the training for Nondual Voyaging. At the same time, even if you have not had contact with Impersonal Movement, please read the paragraphs below. Though some of the paragraphs that refer to Impersonal Movement will not apply to you specifically, you will find that the attitude and help this section offers can be applied to any practice you might be doing on a regular basis. For example, one type of Zen meditation is called shikantaza *and means to "only sit" or to "only sit whole-heartedly." When one does shikantaza (or insight meditation or frankly, any practice (e.g., yoga, qi gong, writing, painting, making music, etc.), one will come up against prior images and thoughts about what the practice "should" be or feel like. In other words, the secret army of the unhealed ego's minions are always operating to keep us from straying too far into the unknown! The paragraphs below are meant to keep any practice fresh, not by squashing the ego's attempt to keep us safe, but instead by simply reminding us to be aware of the drama that is part of the totality of our being.*

Centered Space

1. This is the first in a series of exercises, many of them based on a reframing of some aspects of Impersonal Movement, which will help the student of nondual voyaging maintain contact with the state of consciousness that is necessary for working from this perspective.

2. The practice of Impersonal Movement 1 and 2 is an ideal vehicle for entering into this consciousness. Specifically, within the practice, the stage of Pharaonic Postures at the end of Impersonal Movement 2 can be of great assistance.

3. This variation or addendum to the practice is specifically for students of nondual voyaging. It is not for those who are practicing IM for other purposes. Please take this prohibition seriously.

4. The attitude of someone practicing IM for shamanic purposes is quite specialized and different from the usual approach: here, we *become* illusion. What does this mean?

5. Previously, we have underscored the fact that IM is an "eyes-opened" practice.

6. In other words, we did not want to encourage a dream-like space in which the practitioner's own neurotic/imaginal/escapist thinking could prevail or remain intact. The whole idea was to bring this new understanding and experience of reality into the waking state so that we came out of trance instead of

leaving our ego and its defenses as they were, thus perceiving from that egoic trance some altered or entertaining state that could be co-opted into reinforcing the limited ego's universe.

7. Now, our aim is different.

8. In order to achieve this, the student must be working hard to honestly see the ways in which they protect the ego—knowingly and surreptitiously—trying hard to keep their ego-self as they know it and feel comfortable with it, intact.

9. We simply cannot do these voyaging practices if we are still involved in our feelings and self-importance from a small, egoic point of view.

10. Our actual importance and preciousness only becomes apparent as we are released from the small view.

11. It goes without saying that even if we are practiced in the correct attitudes, we will fail time and again. Yet, we have to have experienced what it is like to be transparent, invisible, without recourse, empty and connected to the *continuity;* we have to have had an experience—even if it is only for a moment—of seeing the world non-conceptually, to take these further steps.

12. When we have had that experience and know that reality is a combination of syntax and beauty, one in which there is a great equality among all manifest and unmanifest things, along with the simultaneous reality

Please think of this state as ordinary rather than rare or dramatic. Most of us have had this experience but perhaps only for brief moments. The voyager practices to make this an accessible, replicable state, not to be sought after as a spiritual high, but to be a fundamental experience the voyager can return to again and again, and one that makes the voyager simpler, smaller and more real. Eventually, it can become a way of life.

of great difference—meaning the unique and precious *is-ness* of each manifest thing—then we can choose to be in the so-called "illusory state" since it is not "illusion" but a *density* in the continuum or *continuity* that makes up all of our reality.

13. Let's restate this in another way: from one perspective, letting go of the trance of neurotic and consensual reality brings us out of the dream, into a grounded reality.

14. Here we are fully responsible for our behavior. This is obviously a completely necessary step for the spiritual aspirant.

15. Now however, our idea of what is "real" and what is "not real" has changed.

16. Since we are using the understanding of *continuity/density* as the vehicle for our relationship with reality, we might reframe our understanding of reality to include dreams—not only as symbolic imagery from our own or the collective unconscious—but as a co-arising part of the single reality, which for us at that moment is simply less vivid or dense.

17. From this perspective we can say that "dreams are going on all the time, whether our consciousness is in a sleep or aroused state" and that the brain doesn't produce dreams at a specific time, but rather produces them all of the time.

    Though it is true that EEGs will show the predominance of certain brain waves at different times, all the various waves are present at all times, but in different states of vividness or *density*.

18. We are simply not engaged with that type of reality during our waking hours. But: we could be.

19. We could choose to integrate that form and level of consciousness if we are free to choose, not because we have become megalomaniacs who feel entitled to do anything we want, but because we have become humble enough by seeing that even our personal self is a creation of the All and is not personally-owned. Or to put it this way: there is no "person" to "own" anything.

20. Ownership has become an outdated frame in which to view this expanded vision of reality.

21. In Impersonal Movement, we go through a series of movements in relationship to specific states of consciousness that are pre-determined. We allow ourselves to "fit into" this new container. We choose to do that.

22. In the same way, aspects of consciousness that some might term "illusory" are simply aspects that have less density for us in a particular state.

23. From the perspective of *continuity/density*, illusion—in the way we are using it, that is, not in the sense of self-deception—should be redefined as a different sense of reality.

24. In this case, the "different sense" is one in which the personal ego is much more transparent (does this make the personal ego "illusory?" Yes. Does it continue to be "real" as well? Yes.)

25. This illusory body and its accompanying mental body images, its abilities, its relationship to time and space and so on, is

> It is the same thing in many meditations, especially those that do not have a stated goal or particular insight as a desired end. In less "constructed" meditations such as Zen's *shikantaza*, who is to say what mental state is correct?

the state of consciousness that is at home in the landscape of *bucolic mind.*

26. It is the proper vehicle for traveling through the landscape, the *everywhere* that the nondual voyager must travel through. And because it is nondual, it heals the voyager as it helps heal the client.

27. As we travel through the landscape of IM, we are tuning our consciousness to another dimension or, better, to have access to additional dimensions.

28. It should be understandable why we would never present the practice of IM in this way to beginners—or even those practicing it to ground themselves more fully in nondual reality.

29. It is very, very easy for a beginner, or even ourselves, to mistake entry into this illusory dimension as some sort of personal excursion into a new realm where the hidden, as-of-yet, un-healing ego is still the king or queen.

30. In the case of those people—and ourselves when we are those people—this nondual shamanic work would create obstacle upon obstacle. Endless trouble.

31. But for those who are ready to take a deeper step into "non-being," or at least non-being from the point of view of the ego's limited notion of what being is, this work only enhances the ability to live and work from a nondual perspective and is essential for nondual journeying.

Pharaonic Postures

1. The Pharaonic Postures—one of the stages of *Impersonal Movement 2*—can be one of the several gateways to the awakening dream-body (illusory body, so-called). We will discuss other gateways later on in this section.

2. To understand this approach we first need to talk at some length about *linguistic space* and *numeric space*.

3. In the Impersonal Movement Manual, I said:

    I wrote in my journal: "A willow grows near the pond because it likes water. But what is this "likes" made of? Chemicals? But what makes these chemicals acquaphilic? Number can only describe this happening: the original impulse must be identical to word.

4. As my spiritual research went on, I became uncomfortable with this characterization of number as something "less than."

5. It was true that art of all types was best described by its connection and emulation of *linguistic space*, but it was also true that when that art materialized from an idea to a fact, number played a role.

6. In a talk I gave about the MAGI Process,[*] I said this:

---

[*] Jason Shulman, *The MAGI Process: A Nondual Method for Personal Awakening and the Resolution of Conflict*, Foundation for Nonduality, 2016, can be purchased at either The Foundation for Nonduality (www.nonduality.us.com) or on Amazon.

So it is the MAGI Process, which gets its power from art (or linguistic space) and not only number.

This curved, intimate thing, which has no characteristics of its own and is colorless and odorless, and without space and time, is intimate itself with the other great organizing scheme of this universe: number.

Number—although it seems abstract—is actually the initial home of the personal. Number separates one thing from another. It names. It catalogs. It marshals forces. It makes things happen. It is me and you.

Linguistic space, on the other hand, makes nothing happen. But nothing would happen without its foundation. The entire physical world emulates and copies this curving moment. It is the soundless hum at the bottom of every sound. The dark light at the foundation of every brightened thing. The concept of fragrance itself without thinking of the rose.

The two together are the founding mother and father of our world and are the creative agencies that make, literally make, our world.

The MAGI Process embodies these two streams and consequently, brings us deeply into the creative process that makes things happen in our world. It is both the circuit and the power source, just as we are both the manifestation of the world and the ones who experience it.

7. The MAGI Process had informed my understanding of the need for both Mother and Father, for *linguistic* and *numeric space*,

for the impersonal *and* personal perspectives.

8. As I continued my work, I began to see that *numeric space* actually appeared in intimate contact with *linguistic space* as the *nodes* I spoke of before:

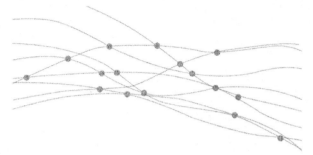

9. Please notice that, in this visual metaphor, linguistic space cannot avoid creating nodes (which are *densities* or individual things, beings and so on, by its very existence. In other words, *densities* and the *continuity* (the same as *linguistic space,* the word we use in Impersonal Movement, are mutually co-arising. They cannot be separated. They are completely nondual. In Buddhism, this is called "dependent arising." One only exists because of the other.*

10. Other examples I created years ago using semi-precious stones. I was not trying at that time to illustrate this concept, but rather, in a deep meditative state, placed these stones and made these connecting lines based on an instinctual feeling of what was true and real to me.

---

* Here is another example: the word *high*—though we think it has meaning independently of anything else, actually has no meaning at all except as it is compared to the word *low*. We know something is high because something else is low. In the same way, we understand the concept of "background" only because there is a "foreground." *Continuity* creates the opportunity for *densities*. But *densities* also create the *continuity*. Truly nondual.

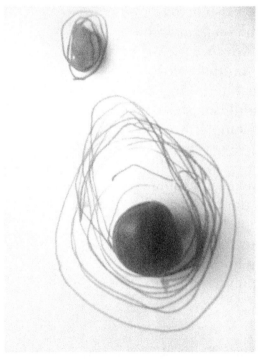

11. At each point where strands of *linguistic space* cross each other, the temporary stillness we could call "a thing," or "a being," has a place to exist. This was a forerunner to the understanding of both *linguistic space* and *nodes* and finally to *continuity/density*.

12. These structures illustrate the creation of a *location* in the boundaryless continuum of *linguistic space*.

13. Consequently, there are an infinite number of nodes because the *continuity* is endless.

14. This is, of course, just a useful metaphor and should not be taken as the way things actually are. An example: since *linguistic space* (or the *continuity*) does not have actual "strands" (just a useful metaphor), we could find other ways of describing or illustrating the interaction between parts of *linguistic space* or even the co-arising of *linguistic space* with *number*. (Please remember that people have different learning styles, inclinations and predilections. Please use my metaphors to explore your own understanding, and please work to feel it in your body.)

15. While conscious awareness of *linguistic space* expands, connects and diffuses, contact with *numeric space* embodies and locates. This is emblematic of some of the differences between IM1 and IM2.

16. If we were to call *linguistic space* "dreamlike," then we would have to call *numeric space* spatial, geometric (as opposed to the essentially a-spatial aspect of *linguistic space* . . .) and specific.

17. While it is possible to avoid characterological problems as we relate to either *numeric space* or *linguistic space*—*exclusively*—because we are in some sense either avoiding the absolute or the relative plane, if we hold awareness of both of these creative elements, all egoic problems will rise to the surface.

18. So the student must always be ready to deal with psychological problems honestly as they occur.

19. It is at the stage of the *Pharaonic Postures* that it becomes possible to interact—and thereby change our consciousness—with the truly unitive state of *linguistic* and *numeric space*. The true holism.*

    The Pharaonic Postures in Impersonal Movement

20. To arrive at the Pharaonic Postures, the student has gone through the entirety of IM 1 and IM 2. The change in consciousness is profound.

21. What sets the stage for the Pharaonic Postures is the intimate and slow contact with *linguistic space*. The practitioner, in other words, has slowed down enough so that it becomes possible to stop all physical movement without losing contact with any portion of *linguistic space*.

22. Only two things are now necessary to experience, and be changed by, what I am calling "Centered Space."

---

* The Pharaonic Postures are an integral part of Impersonal Movement 2. Please see my earlier footnote for a description of this moving, unifying work.

23. The first is to realize that the Pharaonic Posture is a node. It is the place where the personal-without-a-history as a physical posture is realized.

24. As I mentioned in the section entitled "The Silent Body":

    We could say that "The Silent Body" is about emptiness appearing in form, a rather astounding thing! Of course, this notion destroys the concept of "emptiness" being "nothingness," and rather elevates it to the experience of having things, forms and beings in the world to which we can relate from a non-conceptual perspective. This type of consciousness returns our experience of the manifest world to simplicity and light.

25. This is even more true of the Pharaonic Postures: they are embodied emptiness.

26. Far from being an actual stopping-place, this node is a harmonic moment in a sea of change. It is a moment of the coming-out-of-unity into manifestation. It is a first moment and a last moment, an ongoing moment and a unique, single moment in time and space.

27. It is at this point that the practitioner must engage with what the Tibetans call "self-blessing."

28. The practitioner sees himself or herself as a blessing. Literally.

29. You say to yourself as you hold the posture: *I am a blessing.*

30. Doing this will bring up what I called in my notebook "a great, benign stance," and give the student a deep sense of the interrelated web of life with no goal and no owner.

31. The dream-body or the *everywhen-body* is now a vehicle in full contact with both *linguistic* and *numeric space*.

32. The consciousness that is achieved by this *turn* is the consciousness the nondual voyager needs for his or her daily work.

Steps for Pharaonic Postures

1. Do all of IM 1 and IM 2 diligently . . . and with a sense of play!

2. When you arrive at the Pharaonic Postures, remember that you are now in—and are itself—a *node* in *linguistic space*. This *node* is *numeric space*.

3. Holding this realization will change the experience of being in a Pharaonic Posture.

4. Now, proceed with *self-blessing*.

5. Actually say to yourself: *I am a blessing*.

6. This will give you the experience of Centered Space, a fully-radiative, non-personally-owned, warm spaciousness.

7. This is one way to experience what it is like to have made the *turn*.

8. You must still find your own way to this state. This is an example.

Walking Through the Densities

1. Impersonal Movement affords us yet another opportunity to experience the being-state of *the turn*.

2. Please note again that this is for the advanced practitioner, someone who is practicing IM often and consistently.

3. In this practice, after making space solid and relating to the densities outside, *we walk through the densities instead of allowing the densities to move us.*

4. Even though *walking through the densities* occurs right near the beginning of practice, I am assuming that, since you are a practiced veteran, even at the beginning of the practice, you are "deeply into" the consciousness of the practice.

5. *Walking through the densities* is an infinite proposition: There is no end to densities. Yet, you do have the sense of moving from one to the other, as if there were a demarcation between bands or clouds of densities, a metaphor we use as we practice IM. This metaphor has now been softened or enlarged to help the nondual voyager mediate this new environment.

Steps for Walking Through the Densities

1. Begin your practice.

2. Do Forgetting-Remembering deeply.*

3. Don't rush through, thinking you "know" this state and therefore do not have to go step-by-step through the details.

4. Make space solid. We also call this "making space full." It is essentially the same thing: we are confirming and experiencing the fact that every "empty thing" needs a "solid thing," to be empty . . . and vice versa.

5. Space is filled with the activity of this relationship.

6. Space is completely relational.

7. The densities will now appear.

8. Allow yourself—as in the traditional approach to IM practice—to be moved by the densities. Do not give this step short shrift.

9. At some point, start walking through the densities, keeping contact with and awareness of the densities at every moment.

10. You are not walking around the densities or walking into a seam. There are no seams.

---

* "Forgetting-remembering," "walking through the densities," "making space solid," "volition-desire," are all part of Impersonal Movement (IM). The Nondual Voyager must learn IM to set the stage for fully participating in voyaging. IM should only be taught by an authorized teacher of this practice. For information about future Impersonal Movement classes, contact IM@societyofsouls.com.

11. You are walking *through the densities* as if you were walking through a fog. They are continuous.

12. Try this both with your eyes open and eyes closed. If you are doing it with your eyes closed, at some point stop your movement through the densities and simply look at the world around you.

13. You don't forget about the densities, but experience them fully as you walk through them.

14. As before: this is one way to experience what it is like to have made the *turn*.

15. The *turn,* in this case, is the way you prepare yourself to drop into the state of consciousness that allows you to do this.

16. You must still find your own way to this state. This is an example.

Meditation of the Pure Subjective

1. If there is an overall theme to this book about nondual voyaging, it is this: *how can we see beyond our conditioning in order to allow a more deeply integrated vision of reality to enter our lives and work?*

2. *Continuity/density*, the concept of features and featurelessness, bucolic mind, hypnogogic imagery and the understanding of the implications of a single world, are all designed to open the gates of perception so that the world as it is and our participatory involvement can become apparent.

3. We could say that much of the study the voyager does is to acquire the ability to "put everything on the table," in other words, to *locate* all things interior and exterior so that they are not invisible and atmospheric, but present, findable and ultimately helpful.

4. When something is apparent, when it is seen, it can be used. We can enter the totally creative, two-way street—the relational avenue that reality actually is.

5. When something, let's say certain thoughts and feelings, experiences and early childhood trauma, for example, are *not located*, they still exist in the bodymindspirit but are miasmatic, a drop of ink made pale by its expression into water so that it is invisible, part of the ordinary current of events.

6. Nevertheless, this hue colors everything, and because it is unseen, it becomes a

Suggestion: Write the words in the first paragraph that are in *italics* on a small piece of paper and paste it on your bathroom or bureau mirror. It will do wonders for your practice.

central figure in our perception of our self, others, and the world in general.

7. Approaching our own lives and the lives of our clients from the perspective of having located all of who we are frees us, even as some of these miasmatic hues and colorations still exist. In other words, we experience freedom *with*, rather than freedom *from*. This allows for a new level of healing in our self and, eventually, in others whom we work with. We can do what we know.

Freedom

8. The nondual perspective, on one hand, is simply a new metaphor or syntax through which to make sense of the world. On the other hand, each deeper metaphor is a deeper look into reality and, because of that, reveals more of its structure *and* more of our own abilities, many of which were invisible or neglected.

9. When we are truly in a nondual, relational consciousness, we cannot soil our environment so easily since our environment *is our self*. When we are truly in a nondual, relational consciousness, we cannot as easily ignore the needs of other people since other people *are our own self*.

10. Because time is seen only linearly in our usual consciousness, things that seem to be separated by snowdrifts of time are often seen as non-connected. But the nondual voyager lives in a pool of time, one that includes linear time but also one that sees and experiences time as a seamless whole, wherein time resides not as an abstraction

but as physical objects themselves, the ongoing existence of which *is* time itself.

11. For the nondual voyager, all considerations, mental, physical, emotional and so on, are these sorts of objects, objects that contain time, *are* time. Voyagers allow themselves to experience every object as *all of time*. So the past is happening now, the future too. After all, where could these things, the past and future, actually be? Only in this moment of total presence, of total oneness.

12. So these sections—the previous one, which describes a bit of the discipline of Impersonal Movement, and the following meditation—are here to break the pattern of consensus. What is real? And real for whom? And for when? We are not dealing with fantasy here: we are dealing with freedom. We are learning about the freedom to choose syntaxes for our lives, based on kindness and skillful means, a choosing that takes courage on the part of the nondual voyager.

> A nondual voyager is not free from syntax—that is impossible. Our eyes are a syntax, our hands, our brains, our hearts, our bodies. But within certain parameters, a nondual voyager is awake to their syntax and thus is free to choose which syntax to be in.

13. It takes courage to "leave our family" of consensual reality and explore a new one on the other shore, a shoreline that is right here, but goes unnoticed because of the needs of whatever society and time we find ourselves in at the moment.

14. The nondual voyager is a bridge between worlds or, more exactly, one who announces that no bridge is needed since the world is totally connected and accessible.

15. To speak for a moment about the meditation that follows, as we approach this new state, questions such as *Is this real? Is this my imagination?* and others of the same ilk are no longer entertained as real questions, or as questions we can find the answers to if we remain in the same frame of reference. They are leftovers, echoes of a consciousness that depended solely on the subject/object dichotomy as the only reference point from which to decide what was authentic or not.

16. Since all opposites appear in the nondual voyager's world at the same time, not in opposition to each other but as "things in themselves," it is possible to examine each opposite from a new perspective, one in which each former member of a pair of opposites now stands forth freely, allowing its truer nature to be revealed in and of itself.

17. This is the nature of "self-illumination:" each object, thing, thought, feeling and so on, is a portal to the *continuity/density*. Even more than that, much more, each object *is* the *continuity/density itself,* a lamp unto itself but one that is simultaneously connected to every other source of light.

    Question: Who is the one who takes a match to light the lamp?

    Answer: The one who already knows what light is.

18. In this section we are going to explore a form of the subjective that is not simply the other pole of *subject* and *object* but one that is a gateway to the entire universe because it is expressing its true nature. It is best experienced by doing the meditation below.

19. Doing this meditation is somewhat daring as it asks the unhealed parts of our ego—

which are always on the watch-out for anything suspicious—to lift their metaphorical feet and free the ego to fly above its own narrow view, asking questions it has never asked and allowing itself to experience something new. It challenges deeply held beliefs and even more important mental structures that have organized the world and our perception along certain rigid lines.

20. The end result of this meditation, when done from time to time over a long period of time, is a kind of relaxation from the grip of separateness, a holding on that is the result of the unhealed ego's belief that it is in constant danger. This meditation, in other words, gives back some of the agency and spaciousness we were meant to have.

Walking to the End of the Universe

Please read and do this meditation several times a week:

Every day I walk to the end of the universe and there I get into trouble. Wherever your universe is, if you are willing to walk to the end of it, you will get into trouble. If you are willing to be in trouble you will get to walk to the end of the universe the next day. If this is not your intention, then each day you walk the same universe over and over again, like a sleepwalker. But to be awake means to walk to the end of the universe and get in trouble. That could take five minutes or five hours or five days or five months, but you will get in trouble because you will reach the end of your knowledge. You will reach the end of your ability. You will reach the end of your capacity and you will be in trouble. Then if you are willing to sit with that difficulty, embrace that difficulty, touch that difficulty, kiss, make love to that difficulty, whatever level you are willing to do it on—some days you will just want to wave to it, some days you will want to move in with it depending upon how you are doing—then you take that trouble which is now transformed into more universe. It gets transformed into more universe and off you go.

I can't resist putting a word or two in here: We don't need to "go mad." For Jung, a straight-laced Swiss, a resident of a certain milieu, to even think in certain ways was "crazy." Jung was a man of his time, but his greatness of heart makes him a man of our time, too. His huge and courageous heart asked him to go wherever it must to find his truth. And he did.

Let's get into trouble:

21. You begin meditating.

22. In the back of your mind you are remembering a nice feeling you had the

other day, an experience of connection: *this is your own thought.*

You continue . . .

23. You have other spiritual thoughts about what you'll achieve or understand about this universe . . .

24. You wonder if you are awakening or getting a little bit of enlightenment: *this is your own thought . . .*

25. You wonder about nondual voyaging: this is your own thought. There is no voyaging that is not your own thought. Your thoughts about voyaging or God, or the Divine Mother or even reality itself . . . whatever . . . are only your own thoughts and not them themselves at all.

You continue . . .

26. You go through many thoughts and concepts and beliefs and, one by one, you own them, identify them as *only your own thought*. There is no "there" there!

27. Then you search further: you find, in the back of your mind, the slight fragrance of an expectation, an expectation that "things will get better," or that "you will have insight," or just the expectation itself: *even this is your own thought. There is nothing else but your own thought.*

28. No "objective" universe.

Continue to sit there . . .

29. At some point, you will simply feel like yourself, sitting there. This is when the next movement begins . . .

30. Here is a passage from C. G. Jung's *Red Book:*

   > *My soul spoke to me in a whisper, urgently and alarmingly: "Words, words, do not make too many words. Be silent and listen: have you recognized your madness and do you admit it? Have you noticed that all your foundations are completely mired in madness? Do you not want to recognize your madness and welcome it in a friendly manner? You wanted to accept everything. So accept madness too. Let the light of your madness shine, and it will suddenly dawn on you. Madness is not to be despised and not to be feared, but instead you should give it life."*
   >
   > *I: "Your words sound hard and the task you set me is difficult."*
   >
   > *S: "If you want to find paths, you should also not spurn madness, since it makes up such a great part of your nature."*
   >
   > *I: "I didn't know it was so."*
   >
   > *S: "Be glad that you can recognize it, for you will thus avoid becoming its victim. Madness is a special form of the spirit and clings to all teachings and philosophies, but even more to daily life, since life itself is full of craziness and at bottom utterly illogical . . . . life itself has no rules . . . .*
   >
   > and further on . . .

I: "I couldn't find the way"

He says: "You don't need to find a way now."

He speaks the truth. The way, or whatever it might be, on which people go, is our way, the right way. There are no paved ways into the future. We say that it is this way, and it is. We build roads by going on. Our life is the truth that we seek. Only my life is the truth, the truth above all. We create the truth by living it . . .

31. Jung had his "madness." We have our own problems, whatever we call them. When we do the Pure Subjective Meditation, we invite the Universe into relationship with our selves.

32. "*This is your own thought.*" What is behind all of that?

33. A pathless land where choosing who we are is exactly the same as *seeing* who we are.

The Sense of Primordial Space

1. Here is a quote from Chögyam Trungpa and Francesca Fremantle* from their book on understanding the *Tibetan Book of the Dead*:

    Space is emptiness and luminosity: luminous emptiness. Because it is empty, nothing exists, yet because it is luminous, everything arises from it.† *As Trungpa Rinpoche said, the dharmakaya (the formless state of being) arises unnecessarily out of the infinite space. Here there is neither samsara nor nirvana, neither self nor other, neither Buddhas nor sentient beings. This state is known as primordial purity because it is not stained or obscured by any hint of confusion or dualistic thought; it is the original, pure nature of all existence, which always remains at the heart of all apparent phenomena.*

2. Trungpa Rinpoche's words here might mislead people, however. Certainly, for the purposes of the voyager, they can easily mislead one into thinking that this world of "unstained purity" is the one we are after. This is not true at all. We are after "stained purity" if you will!

---

* Chögyam Trungpa and Francesca Fremantle, *The Tibetan Book of the Dead: The Great Liberation Through Hearing in the Bardo*, Shambhala Classics, 2000.
† Please compare this to the first stage of Impersonal Movement where we "make space solid," or "full." This is another way of talking about the luminousness of space. As the quote continues, I am hesitant to agree with Trungpa's traditional associations with the dharmakaya because it is easy, from passages such as this, to think that the dharmakaya could exist independently—as if it stood on its own with its own independent being. This would make the idea of primordial purity very attractive to an ego that is in the pain of existence. I tend to shy away from notions of purity because as attractive though they are, they are not reliable friends.

3. As Trungpa says, *[in this state] there are neither Buddhas nor sentient beings.*

4. I bring this up simply to contrast the difference between the experience of contacting primordial space (or the absolute alone without its personal face) in its traditional setting and the avenues through which the nondual voyager needs to explore, which is through our understanding of *quality*.

5. The experience of primordial space as described in Tibetan sources relates to a specific *experience*. While it is an important experience to have along the spiritual journey, the nondual shaman wants to go where there *are* Buddhas and sentient beings.

6. In other words, the voyager walks directly into the world of duality because *there is no hierarchy between linguistic* or *numeric space* (Impersonal Movement terms) or, as we say now, *continuity* and *density*. This means that the relationship is not linear, but simultaneous: one does not create the other but, rather, each makes the other possible.

7. There is no higher or lower.

8. In Buddhist terms, I would say that the *dharmakaya* is not prior (in temporal terms) to anything. It is not "the mother" of anything since the mother exists only because of the existence of the child.

9. To state it another way, *linguistic space* (synonymous here with the *continuity*), which like the *dharmakaya* is indeterminate

in nature, is not the basis for the determinate aspects of life such as *numeric space*, but more of a twin, born at the same moment, each a "twin" only because of the existence of the other.

10. So for the nondual voyager, to walk into primordial space *is* to walk into the world of men and women, dogs and cats, to walk into manifestation. There is nothing but this manifestation no matter how much we try to make believe there is something separate.

11. Said another way, while there is a difference of feeling between the characterless land of *continuity* and the specificity of the manifest world (the *densities*), all of manifestation appears as that state we call *quality*, which owes its existence to both this characterless continuity and its concurrent, co-arising manifestations. You just can't get away from it.

12. The luminosity that is primordially present comes from this union and nothing else. *Continuity* <u>and</u> *density*. Because this is so, men and women, mountains and streams shine *as* light and not because they are illuminated by something else.

13. The nondual voyager is most interested in the play of duality and its manifestations.

14. This is his or her chosen field of play.

15. I would like to restate all of this in another way, so that we can relate directly to the job the voyager has chosen.

16. To relate to *linguistic space* (or the *continuity*) alone is misleading.

17. Without relating to *numeric space* (or *densities)* simultaneously, the nondual voyager will accidentally (secretly?) keep their ego intact and unchanged.

18. Why is this? Because by relating to the *continuity-alone*—even though this is an important experience to have—the egoic problems of being an individual tend to fade and even disappear, giving the student the idea that all is well. Well, all is *not* well. That is part of human life as well.

19. In deep contact with *the absolute-alone*, the ego disappears . . . instead of being *healed*.

20. It is very possible to have a profound connection to the *continuity-alone* and other non-egoic states, and still be an idiot.

21. Nondual voyagers cannot afford to be idiots. They can be fools; they can be wild and artistic or dull or precise. But they cannot be unintegrated or unaware.

22. (Please remember that any state, when sequestered or separated from any other—such as *density-alone*, will bring a different, but similar problem with it and not the true wholeness the person desires.)

23. For me, nondual awareness is not based on either this characterless ground of being or on the manifestations of duality that spring unbidden from it. Instead, it is both. Always. Without hierarchy or preference.

> Let me contradict myself here. Instead of "without hierarchy or preference," how about *with hierarchy and preference*? But then, that preference itself must be "on the table," so to speak. If it is not, it becomes actualized and lived out. But when it is "on the table," it is simply another interesting *feature* of reality, another tree or pond or friend you wave to from across the street.

24. Though we need to have an experience of the unimpeded absolute or *dharmakaya*, the experience of awakening into nondual awareness is one of having both worlds as a single manifestation.

25. My position is that nondual awareness, instead of being free from confusion and egoic trials and dualistic thinking, is *completely aware of them even as they (might) happen or occur within the bodymindspirit of imperfect beings.*

26. By subtly making *two states,* that of the primordial space and that of dualistic thinking and so on, this point of view does not emphasize that the relative world and the absolute one *must arise together simultaneously.*

27. There is no primordial space without the differentiated world, the relative plane.

28. They are not two different things but sun and sunlight, gold and yellow, breath in and breath out.

> Or: Wax on! Wax off! (Please see *The Karate Kid,* 1984.)

29. They do not arise *in time* but *create time* by their co-arising.

30. Why all of this is important is because all of the exercises we will do together are not searching for some primordial state, but for that state that shows up when *linguistic* and

numeric space are united, when the absolute and the relative are united, when *continuity* is united with *density*.

31. This is our gateway into dream-body, dream-time or, put another way, the underlying strata of our world, that is truly mixed everywhere and *everywhen* the nondual voyager calls home.

32. This is an important difference. This is how we get our hands dirty in the illuminated muck of the world.

33. This combined awareness of the undifferentiated aspect and the relative plane is a different space than relating to either of them as a single "place."

34. This is the operating theater of the nondual voyager.

35. I must admit that it is also much more difficult to maintain this stance since there is no end to being an idiot! This is something we all are at different times.

36. The moment that one can see their own idiocy arise and still maintain their awakening state is the moment that a Buddha (or true shaman!) *and* a sentient being (or a true voyager!) arise together in a single person who goes forth to help and heal.

37. In this next exercise we will be gazing at a picture of aperiodic or "non-periodic" tiling. For many of us, it will be a visual/body experience of being in *continuity* and *density* at same time.

38. The mathematics of aperiodic tiling are far beyond my understanding. But I chose this picture because it seemed intuitively to me to combine both *linguistic* and *numeric space,* which is to say *continuity/density.*

39. By gazing at this pattern, the brain is somehow thwarted in its pattern-making ability and desire and, instead, gazes into something that cannot be reduced to anything else.

40. For me, it opens a doorway into the *turn.* It is not exactly the same, but we could say it is a rehearsal for the real thing.

41. Please see if it does that for you.

42. Remember to keep breathing as you gaze at this diagram.

Ammann bars

The Living and the Dead

1. The voyager's territory—a land where *continuity/density* is both the name of our darkness and our light—could be likened to the space between life and death.

2. Here, rather than talking about actual physical death, we will be dealing with transitional space as emblematic of *life and death within the world of our conscious awareness.*

3. In other words, we are looking toward transitional space as a doorway—a "thin place" between the worlds—where we can enter as a physical presence, as a healer.

4. In our situation and cultural context—unlike traditional shamans who often use psychoactive drugs or extended drumming or dancing to momentarily change consciousness, thus allowing themselves access to other continuums of *density*—we must continually face questions as to who we are on both the unitive and relative levels of being. This is part of our ongoing practice.

5. We must be committed to both improving our constant state of imperfection and inviting all of our basic imperfections gratefully into the family of our being.

    > No more orphans standing outside the door, asking to come in.

6. We are grateful for these imperfections because—although the unhealed portions of our egos do not like them and are often threatened by them—they stand as keyholes through which we can look at and

eventually consciously participate in the brightness that is our true home.

7. Our unhealed and unintegrated egos are, as I have mentioned, primarily interested in survival. This is part of their righteous job and also, because it is a narrow view of life, part of the deficiencies of a life lived with only that end in mind.

8. So, since life is radically impermanent, utterly devoid of dependable constancy, this bedrock feature is usually seen as only a threat to survival, and we consequently miss the resources and richness brought by this radical impermanence exemplified by *life and death in every moment.*

9. In the view of the nondual shaman, the great transitional state of life and death is our ally, especially when we do not focus on ultimate physical death alone, but instead focus on the falling into small deaths that accompany every moment of living.

10. Because *death,* viewed in this manner, is a transitional space, it is important for each of us to explore what our attitude is toward *all* transitional spaces, since—as I mentioned above—in addition to the major transitions we all experience in life, the innate, radical impermanence of life causes a sort of transitional vibration through each and every moment of our day.

    Please remember that learning all of these paradigms and conditions of nondual voyaging do not have to happen sequentially. There is a nonlinear (yet still developmental) path as well. We come to some stages and insights sooner . . . and some, later.

11. Eventually, the voyager will use, or ride, this vibratory condition in order to make radical connections and associations that might not be possible or even noticed if associative

thinking were limited to psychological space alone.

12. While in our daily life, relating to these spaces is often ignored in favor of quotidian moments, for voyagers this is exactly where we want to go.

13. This is the world the voyager lives and works in. It is the place where the world unbinds itself and flows over its boundaries and reveals its flowing and fertile nature.

14. It is a truism that we cannot go someplace we are not willing to go.

15. Depending upon the state of our egoic integration, trying to enter these cracks between the worlds will be prohibited to the extent that we are afraid of change.

Entering the gates

16. If our defensive structure is activated by change, or if it is put solely in the service of our unhealed ego, these thin places cannot be entered because they are seen as *realms,* which is to say, actual objective domains. In other words, the ego, when it is in its unhealed state, and consequently in a state wherein it thinks of itself as an actual entity with no precursor or antecedent—as an entirely separate being—sees the world made over in its own image. In kabbalistic terms, this would be considered a *yesh* or an "existence."

17. This would underscore or rigidify the unhealed ego's belief that there is a solid, unchanging personal self, a structure or existence with its own domain, which

should resolutely resist change of any sort in order to survive.

18. This ego does not see that change is a way of having ongoing, intimate connection with the world. It does not understand how learning and changing are related or how the flow of information—which is really a form of touching—happens through constant change.

19. Contrary to this, the nondual voyager seeks to see these gateways as the home where the magic and play of the world takes place and where we participate as active members and agents of change.

20. We are both the shoreline that shapes the river and the river that shapes the land, each in its intricate, beautiful and temporary dance.

21. While transitional states upset the status quo and because the human ego is self-charged with keeping homeostasis at all costs ("keeper of the homeostasis" might even be a very good definition of what the ego is), we human beings find transitional states difficult, even life- and sanity-threatening.

22. But these states nonetheless afford us a look through the appearance of things. Through them and our relationship with them, we get to see what is there when our conventional life, life as we know it, with our routines, habits, modes of thinking, hopes and dreams at full-throttle, disappears or fades away or even clears away entirely to show something new.

IYI:
The concept of "self-charged" is structural: a plant is "constructed" to need sunlight. The plant and sunlight are one thing and not two. Similarly, there is no one asking the ego to maintain homeostasis. Ego and homeostasis are a single thing. It is constructed to tell this story. In both cases, the mission or need *is* the thing that seeks it. The structure *is* the path.

23. In a sense, we get to look through the looking-glass to the other side of the mirror.

24. Now, without the obscurations of the established facts of our lives, we not only see the players in the drama of our life—our egos, our conditioning, our fears and longings—but we get a glimpse of the subtle forces and energy-dynamics that make our lives what they are . . . that even make our ego what it is as it heals: a dynamic center, a theme, a view, an organizing principle that seeks out balance and beauty and the true eternal, the ongoing flow of change.

25. *All of this takes place within the framework of duality*, that realm that actually has the highest level of energetic tension because it holds within it—incarnated in a world of matter—thought and body, considered polar opposites in life.

26. The voyager uses this high level of energy—which can be felt to the degree that reality-as-it-is is no longer threatening—to peer into manifestation itself and, through all of this, to help.

27. Inhabiting—and using—this high level of energy is what is needed to evoke change in this recalcitrant kingdom. Please remember the first Step in the MAGI Process:* *First the angry earth plane vectors.*

> This is the true "Returning to the Marketplace," the last stage of the Ten Ox-Herding pictures. But instead of a jolly, fat Buddha with a hobo's satchel over his shoulder and children gathered around him—quite an idealistic picture of the bodhisattva's work!—the nondual voyager finds him or herself standing in traffic in Times Square, hopefully still fat and happy!

---

* The MAGI Process (*The MAGI Process: A Nondual Method for Personal Awakening and the Resolution of Conflict*, Shulman, The Foundation for Nonduality, 2016)—a thirty-eight-step, spiritually dynamic methodology for the resolution of conflict and awakening—is a way of participating in the creative machinery of the world. Since, from a nondual perspective, we are part of the world, made by the world and simultaneously *making* the world, to do the Process is to engage fully with reality. It is to drop into the programming language that made and makes the world as we know it.

28. When we are not trying to "make everything nice," but allowing the clash of matter to operate according to the laws of this realm, the resulting energies can be an agent of and vehicle for change. Of course, we must be willing to invite these conditions into our conscious awareness first.

29. The voyager does not automatically pursue reconciliation or equanimity as the goal. Instead, he or she is interested in the direct illumination that occurs when the entire continuum of the distinct and separate world is allowed to be as it is and we are allowed to be an awakening part of it.

30. Transitions, whether at the moment of death or at the moment of helping ourselves and others, if we are brave enough to use them, don't take us to *another world*, but set us down directly *in this one*, interfacing us directly with the energies that draw and shape us.

31. This is where, according to my thinking, the true illumination begins.

32. The Tibetan book *Liberation Through Hearing*, usually referred to more popularly as "The Tibetan Book of the Dead," is a book that describes transitional states of all types, though it is mostly associated with the transitions between physical life and death.

The thirty-eight steps of the MAGI Process are the actual answers about what is really here and who we are. They describe the essence of what you will find at every step of the journey when personal desires and questions come into contact with the great, impersonal vastness of Reality. The first step, mentioned in the text above, acknowledges the fact that *any* change will be resisted by reality's built-in, non-personal inertia. Thus, the beginning of all enterprises of change must take this truth as its starting point and the foundation of the manifest world. It is important to understand that this inertia is not a negative or positive thing. It simply *is*.

This gap or *bardo* is the space between death and re-birth.

33. We see that the Tibetans, in this text, are not separating *life* from *death* in the usual way, that is, by calling *death* "the end of life" and writing a magical-thinking text about what happens from there on in.

34. Instead, they are putting all of this *life-death* thing into a single "continuity," where one part not only leads linearly to another (as in: life *into* death . . .), but also bi-directionally or circularly (as in: *death* into *re-birth* . . .).

35. So this book called *Liberation through Hearing*, and the part of a spiritual student's journey as exemplified by the *bardo* state, is about diving directly into the difficult state of transition, which—though sometimes emblematic of major life changes—is actually taking place, in miniature, all the time.

36. If we relate to these territories of transition from the reference point of our rigidity, fears and habits—in short, the smallest parts of our personality—then the experience of the transitional state can be terrifying and its worth minimal.

37. If we relate to being with them as yet another technique we can own, as in something we can *do* rather than something we must *be*, or something we *are*; if we relate to these territories as something that we can *manage* and be successful with, while remaining unchanged, then the worth of

our experience of the transitional state is—again—minimal.

38. We all start with the possibility of relating to transitional states in a completely positive, open way, which is to say that all we need for both liberation and healing is contained in our native state.

39. What happens next—the arising of fears that cause further levels of diminished consciousness, contractions against energies because we feel personally vulnerable, the falling to lesser and lesser states of consciousness—is of great interest to us as spiritual explorers and healers. Relating to what happens is part of the training of the voyager as well.

40. We don't reject these "fallings" to more limited states as failures because *this is human life too.*

41. This is what we do, despite our vows and hopes to the contrary: we fall and rise, succeed and fail. Viewed in this way, our mixed ability to control our contractions along with our efforts to overcome these limitations, offers an intimate map into our humanity, into each of our personal humanities. Because of that our efforts are not only concentrated on the Olympian spiritual athletes who pass through transitions with the greatest of ease but on the healing each of us needs, a healing that does not deny our humanness and our inabilities.

42. If we do not take in this imperfect feature of life (and ourselves . . .), who can we help?

43. When the nondual shaman can delve into reality with minimal defensiveness, knowledge arises, and trust in the illuminating quality of daily life begins to shine.

44. When the voyager voyaging is not afraid to see what is there, without trying to manipulate what is seen or heard, or make a narrative that is more acceptable to the smallest parts of ourselves, then there is value.

45. This is a moment of direct, face-to-face confrontation with the pure, dynamic energy of existence, the *continuity/density*.

46. But what the nondual voyager studies is not this high point, which happens automatically when we are open to *what-is*, but the limitations themselves, the ancient wars still being fought in each voyager's soul and body and also in the body and soul of every person the voyager wishes to help.

> We want to be greatly enlightened about our delusions.

47. We see these in detail, in ourselves and others.

48. The nondual voyager is someone who is in service to someone else and thus his or her shamanic practice is to be able to integrate all of what he or she is—the greater and the lesser—so that the basic illumination of the situation, which is nondual in origin, can begin to shine.

49. As I have said before, the illumination we are after is not the illumination of purity but the light of the union between background and foreground, between the

absolute stream that everything rides on and the water and sand, currents and waves, communities and settlements that find their homes here along this river of life.

50. The flint and the tinder: illumination comes from the arising of both.

51. Let's be clear: in doing this, the voyager is illuminated. Doing this, the client's situation becomes workable . . . healable.

52. This is what *causes* the shining to be known consciously. This is what awakens us.

53. When we peer into the space between the worlds of life and death, we arrive at the borderland where knowledge—fresh for that moment, fresh for that person—is found.

54. It is not second-hand. Thus, it cannot be taught in the traditional manner but must be found. The training the nondual shaman gets *is how to find, first in themselves and then in others.*

55. As trainees in the world of light, we will all find that our concepts are projected upon what is happening and changing, and these limitations often convince us in one way or another that this experience "will be the death of us."

56. As I intimated: we should expect this and even welcome it.

57. We approach transitions with trepidation for the most part, especially so when they either come out of the blue or were not planned in advance. A divorce, an illness, a

change of living conditions, the loss of a friend either through death or argument, a breaking apart or a putting together: anything that engulfs us in some way, can be seen as threatening to the survival of the being we have come to be.

58. In the book of *Liberation Through Hearing* (called this because a lama is instructed to read this text into the ear of the dead person . . .) this first face-to-face with the most luminous light occurs as the sensory system shuts down.

59. To translate this in an interesting way, we might say that all of our egoic, habitual systems are—for a moment—not available to us, and a Great Transparency takes its place, through which Reality reveals itself, offering us a way into a new experience of what-is.

> Many of our techniques (such as *bucolic mind*) are a way of breaking down, ignoring or ultimately including our habitual egoic systems so that something new can arise.

60. How we see the world depends completely on the filters over the eyes of our soul, our heart, our mind and our being.

61. Where one person might see another as a competitor, another might see that person as a teammate. We might call these tendencies *karma*, and whether it is a genetic propensity or a neurotic one, the point is: reality appears to us as we make it.

62. In his commentary on *Liberation Through Hearing*, Trungpa Rinpoche explained the dying process in terms of the uncertainty, fear and confusion we experience as we go through the stage of dissolution. We are leaving behind the real, solid, dualistic world of the living and entering the unreal,

shifting, ghostly world of the dead: "the graveyard that exists in the midst of the fog." As we would expect, this does not apply only to impending death in the literal sense, but also to the continual occurrence of dissolution in everyday life. Our experience of life is based on duality—self and other, subject and object, good and bad, pleasure and pain; this is the cause of all our confusion. We are programmed in this way by the skandhas (the intertwined sense-aggregates that make up the experience of "our self.") So this mode of experience is what we consider real; it has become the criterion by which we judge reality. When the elements dissolve at death, the whole structure on which our dualistic perceptions of the world is based begins to crumble away, and our sense of identity is undermined.

63. Let me say that this is a wonderful description of the world inhabited by the advanced spiritual student and nondual voyager, day after day, moment after moment.

64. The voyager does his or her work in this borderland, this ghostly place where, being a sort of ghost himself, changed in a heartbeat by the gusts of time, he is unafraid of being met by such a world.

65. In this world, we don't *look for things*, since *looking* would still be keeping "the looker" intact and off to the side. Looking does not allow a new perspective to enter.

66. So instead of looking, *we find what is there.*

67. This is a major difference. As Picasso said about the way he paints: *I do not seek. I find.*

68. When we cannot do this, we keep re-interpreting reality, ultimately with less and less connection to the energy of what is actually happening and more and more connection to our fears.

69. We then see change through the eyes of our karma, our tendencies, our habitual states of thinking and feeling.

70. The idea is not to *not see* reality through these things—after all, they are part of our cellular nature!—but to *know the filters we are looking through.*

71. This is what brings us freedom. This is what is called "being awake."

72. We are not after some form of perfection where our negative thinking, our limitations and egoic concerns, our karma and genetics don't interfere with some imagined pristine vision of what reality is and isn't.

73. Instead we begin to see transitional states as gateways to illumination, as doorways to a reorganization of our lives *into deeper aliveness.*

74. We are allies with all of ourselves, our imperfections, our limitations, our lack of ability, and we see all this through eyes that are awake to what is actually happening.

75. This is the only way to conquer one of the trickiest tendencies we all have: the tendency toward purity as a saving grace.

76. In the path of the nondual voyager, and indeed all of us, whether we are shamans or not, we can only develop ultimate compassion by becoming intimate with our lack of ability.

77. We can only become compassionate healers to all beings by being kind to ourselves as we go through the difficult relationship with the transitional states that are our constant companions in this path of life.

78. I would like to suggest several exercises through which we may be able to begin to use both the major transitional states and the constant impermanence that is part of life's process and purpose.

79. Through this work, we may further define what it means to be a voyager and the territory we must become familiar with to do our job.

Exercises, Conditions, Clothing to Try On

Things to Taste

Some of these exercises are substantial modifications of ancient Tibetan shamanic practices. Others are from my experience alone.

Tasting

1. The taste of a pear. Re-create this in great detail in your mind.

2. The taste of an apple. Re-create this in your mind.

3. Switch from one to the other and back again until you can bring up either at will.

4. Do this every day for a week.

Geography

1. Visualize your bones as mountains. Go further: your bones *are* mountains. Stay with this image and reality.

2. Your blood and lymph, the parts of you that lubricate or emit, your saliva or tears, are rain and gatherings of water. They are identical to brooks and streams, lakes and ponds. Stay with this image and reality.

3. Your bodily openings are *space.* Go methodically through all of them: nostrils and ears and mouth; penis, vagina and anus. Each one of them is space. Stay with this image and reality.

4. Remember to breathe!

5. Your heart is thunder.

6. Rivers are your nerves and *nadis* (subtle spiritual channels).

7. Your excrement is earth. Stay with these images and this reality.

> The mountains and waters of the immediate present are the manifestation of the path of the ancient Buddhas. Because they are the self before the emergence of signs, they are the penetrating liberation of immediate actuality.
> *Mountains and River Sutra, Master Dogen.*

Going out into the territory

Seeing Through Empty Eyes

1. Those fleshy eyes (or ears or nose or body or mind . . .) are still in the purely psychological world, the world of "actor/acted upon."

2. Divine eyes (or ears or nose or body or mind . . .) see the world as-it-is, that is, with the inclusion of the ego as an actor rather than as an identity.

3. This is what is meant by "non-attachment." It is not some egoic version of "self-contained" or "quietude."

4. Instead, it is simply the placing of the ego into the world of actors, rather than the world of beings.

5. Doing this, we see what is *seen* and the act of *seeing as well.*

6. This is what is called "awakened seeing."

7. This "seeing" (or smelling or tasting et al.) is like not seeing at all in the ordinary way, since there is no "being" there.

8. Pick up something to inhale, something to smell, a piece of fruit, a flower, a twig, some earth. But as you sniff, include the sense of smell *itself* and not just its product (the particular fragrance). Do the same with something you see: don't just *see it*, but include your eyes in the seeing. What changes?

9. Do this every two or three days for two weeks.

Solitude: A Consideration

1. Guard your solitude.

2. Then you will not need the protection of your earthly mother.

3. Then you will be lonely but free.

4. From there, you will sing.

5. Your quiet song will raise armies of companions.

6. At this point, your efforts to "tell all" to whomever are an attempt to be held in your mother's arms and be safe.

7. What you hold dearly within *is your solitude*.

8. It is the obsidian stone of your soul.

9. In that place is the stored power of your soul. It emerges on its own as an animal emerges into spring when the frosts are gone.

10. Even then, it is alone—yet interacts with everything and everything acts upon it.

11. It is a mortal crusader, churning with the stuff of life.

12. The Divine Mother notices beings like this.

What Constellation? A Contemplation

1. We follow the patterns in stars and in this way find our way.

2. But stars have no patterns.

3. So where do these life-servicing patterns come from?

4. They come—first—from ourselves.

5. So pay attention to that part of you!

6. But second, who made *our* patterns and thus gave us pattern-making abilities and the ability to save our souls with patterns in the sky?

7. To know "who," you need to stop looking and *see*.

8. "Who" is the Name of all of this.

9. So Who sees patterns in the stars and Who follows them and saves souls.

10. Thus we thank everything that is *Who,* and *Who* is endless, with no beginning or end.

11. Every road is the road to *Who,* and we can be grateful every minute to be alone, for these moments—conscious, awake—are there so we can thank *Who*.

The Collage Metaphor

1. Reading about the collage artist Ray Johnson[*] the other day, I was struck by the fact that "collage" is a perfect metaphor for—or even description of—what the nondual shaman does, both the process he or she goes through, and the result.

2. The route the nondual voyager follows to get to a result is—as in a collage—one in which various, disparate pieces are gathered together and arranged to present something that is beyond the individual images, yet at the same time is completely informed by them and made of their material.

3. Inherent in the nature of collage is contradiction, opposition and communication, as one image is placed upon another.

4. Each image changes its companions as it itself is changed by them.

5. In their overlapping, covering, hiding and showing, images reveal and conceal as a single, simultaneous activity—not in opposition to each other.

6. Collage is beyond time. It is constructed from images that show moments of time but create something that is not about time but rise to a sort of silence, something a-temporal and eternal. Think of Joseph

---

[*] Raymond Johnson (1927-1995) was an innovative New York collage artist and a central figure in the New York art scene during the early Pop art period.

Cornell's object-filled, three-dimensional collage boxes, and you will see this "beyond time" aspect in action.

7. In this way, by this mode of activity, the time-bound becomes unbound. The born becomes un-born and then re-born as the pieces work synergistically to say something that none of the pieces themselves could utter.

8. Both the collage and the practice of the nondual voyager are timeless and time-bound: they are done *in time* for a specific reason and for a particular person, but they reach into a *timeless realm*—which then becomes expressed in time, brought back as healing.

9. Both the collage and the practice of the nondual voyager are solidly physical activities of this world and use the materials of this world. The collagist uses paper, glue, objects, juxtapositions in time and space. The nondual voyager uses his body and mind, his history and thoughts, and the natural world within and outside of him.

10. Yet, both activities are in some way unperturbed by the materials at hand in that they ignore easy associations and "see through" appearances to the heart of things—even *constructing* the heart of things as they go along. Each is an *art*.

11. Both are associative and overlapping, poetic, metaphoric, symbolic and non-symbolic, harmonic and dissonant, since they are both unafraid of difference, dissimilarity and non-congruence. These are, instead, the stuff of creativity. This is the process.

12. Because this process, this art, is in its heart nonlinear and non-scientific, because its causality is not only linear but also nonlinear, bi-directional and even circular—the result is that the voyager's mind is ruminative, suggestible, potent and boustrophedon.*

13. All of this is to say that even the effect upon those we work with as voyagers is in the form of a living collage, layer upon layer of intimate contact with not just a static locality called "a person," but a layered, nuanced, constantly changing, dynamic process that both informs the one we work with and helps create a new person by the power of this dialogue itself.

14. The nondual voyager is liable to give advice or communicate images from the past, present or future equally because time is likewise non-static and not captured by one state of consciousness.

15. In a collage, a historical image or figure or object might be juxtaposed or layered with a present-day image or even an abstraction. Time is malleable, and this malleability reveals leitmotifs and harmonics.

16. Because nondual voyager-shamans are not limited to any particular view, they bring a full palette of possibilities to the one they work with.

---

* From ancient Greek, *boustrophedon* means "like, in the manner of" (that is, turning like oxen in plowing); it is a kind of bi-directional text, mostly seen in ancient manuscripts and other inscriptions. Every other line of writing is flipped or reversed, with reversed letters. Rather than going left-to-right as in modern English, or right-to-left as in Arabic and Hebrew, alternate lines in boustrophedon must be read in opposite directions. Also, the individual characters are reversed, or mirrored. It was a common way of writing in stone in ancient Greece.

17. They might advise or commiserate, contradict or oppose, create or deny, ritualize, simplify or complexify.

18. They help create a new metaphor, which pushes into the unknown and makes way for the new.

19. The voyager—like the collage artist—uses the available material and is not afraid to choose. This choosing is a form of healing as it discerns and discriminates, separating what is useful from what is not.

20. This process uses the material at hand. In other words, it does not seek to find "other worlds" but sees this one in its abundance of paths and ways to heal, and where it needs to be refashioned and revivified.

21. Because *continuity/density* is its guiding principle, interior and exterior, the overtly physical and the subtle, dreamlike and energetic are a single continuum, all experienced by the voyager physically within the body.

22. This is not a thoughtful abstraction but a practice of bones.

23. Ray Johnson created collages that he sent through the mail, asking for additions from the addressee and for the piece to be sent back as further correspondence.

24. In the same way, yet differently, the voyager makes "correspondences," which is to say, *connections* between disparate things. He or she finds the light in the heavy, the torment in the smile, the stillness in the storm.

25. And further: the nondual shaman *makes himself a collage* because he or she understands that he is not a symbol standing metaphorically for the universe, but *is* the universe in its totality.

26. As R.A. Schwaller de Lubicz says:

    ". . . and man is not an image, a condensation of the Universe; man is the Universe."

27. Here is an example from some information I was/and received one day on a voyaging journey for a client. I had made my *turn* and discovered . . . nothing.

28. After understanding that this was not the "nothing of resistance"—something I am familiar with from many of my own spiritual practices!—I saw that I was being thrown inward in a new way:

    . . . be a brother or sister to the earth in your own body. Do not look outside yourself for this earth because the earth is your body, your own body; do not go out of it to visit trees and streams, stones and roads, clouds and rain; all of this is inside since those very things made you. The water inside and the water outside are the same. The clay inside you and the clay on the hillside are the same.

29. So the nondual voyager does not pretend that he or she is a primitive native of some soil but is who he is, now remembering that everything, every element, every combination of things, is within him or herself, the Mother within and without for safekeeping.

30. My interpretation of this was that instead of looking outside (I often gaze into the natural world to take the journeys I take), *I returned all of the natural world into my own body until "outside" and "inside" was a single thing.*

31. In this way I was bound to the world and the world was bound to me.

32. Where is the nondual voyager's home? Where does he reside? The voyager's home is wherever he or she happens to be. And the voyager is not afraid to go where he or she is needed.

33. Living in a world of correspondences, swimming in the spirit of all things, the nondual voyager peers into the world seeking to heal.

The Gift: Making Magic Manifest

1. Charms, amulets and rituals—which we could call gifts—are an act of transmission that the voyager can share with the client.

2. These acts of transmission cannot happen unless the voyager is in a nondual state. Otherwise it's just an expression of goodwill, deep feeling perhaps, all of which is salutary and curative, but not the same thing as transmission.

3. Transmission is not a linear event nor even a temporal one. Though it occurs in space and time, its effect is web-like and nonlinear, and the effects we can attribute to its cause can be greatly separated in time and space. This means the causality of transmission is not linear, nor focused on a single outcome.

4. To transmit, we must have given up—at least to an important degree—the pursuit of success. If we are only looking to say the right thing, make the right thing and speak the right words, we miss the larger picture in which every "wrong" thing, every failure, leads inevitably to a new truth, a truth beyond the polarities of this binary choice.

5. We are looking for the thing that glows.

6. When the voyager has reached the point—or at least has tasted it—where each density, whether it is an object, natural or manmade, every thought and feeling, every moment of being confused or enlightened, of being lost or found, shimmers because it

reveals that it is simply the *continuity* itself in material form, then each *density* (word, action, object or thought) is a portal to transmission.

7. We might say that this transmission is really a transmission of the possibility of a new consciousness arising to enlarge one that is no longer serving a healing purpose.

8. If the shaman is still someone who is attempting to create a spiritual object (or to voyage, for that matter) as an entirely separate person, one who stands off to the side like a powerful creator and observes his or her creation or voyaging as a separate being, then the voyager has not reached the stage in which they can actually create from a nondual point of view.

9. However, when the voyager sees themselves, their body, mind and spirit, their ego, their thoughts positive and negative, as something that is "on the table," something that is a *feature* of the *continuity*, then the possibility of creating true amulets, mystic words, rituals and so on, spiritual events—true magic, if you will—that will not add obstacles to the one the voyager is working for, becomes a possibility.

10. These spiritual objects or events are not symbolic but *actual*. They are self-illuminated, embodied actions—whether they are things that move or things that appear still. They are completely and utterly themselves as separate creations and, simultaneously, connected to everything.

11. When we place all of our *features* "on the table," we begin to see that we, which is to say our very self and everything that this self can do, are not personally-owned. Yet it is also true that within the field of the personal self, within that frame or limited purview in which "personal" is the watchword, the personal self is one-hundred percent responsible for its actions. Not being "personally-owned" is not an excuse for not being accountable for oneself.

12. The voyager who does not seek ownership, yet is fully responsible, is the one who can transmit.

13. We find this level of transmission not only in shamanistic work but in art of all sorts when the art rises to the level of *quality*. When scientists and mathematicians talk about the beauty that resides in an equation or insight, they are talking about this same *quality*.

14. When art rises to the level of *quality*, something is transmitted to the viewer that is beyond the pieces the art is made of, whether these are the assemblage of colors, the shapes and dimensions of a sculpture, the movements of a dance, or the series of notes and silences that go into making music.

15. There is an apprehensible demarcation wherein the artist goes beyond a certain level—let's call it *continuity alone* or *density alone,* (equivalent terms in Impersonal Movement would be *linguistic space alone* and *numeric space alone*) and arrives at a level where *density* is inseparable from *continuity*,

where the materials of the art have been both transcended *and are themselves the continuity.*

16. Then something beyond words, beyond music, beyond dance or art or literature is firmly held in the material world and, in this way, transmitted anew and fresh to each audience member or viewer.

17. This is what moves us.

18. For those of you who have practiced Impersonal Movement, we could say that the gift the voyager gives the client, whether this gift is verbal or something drawn or written or some natural object, happens only as the voyager is seated in the place of *volition-desire.** In addition, the voyager has the added responsibility of knowing that they are voyaging on behalf of another human being.

19. Please contemplate this for a moment!

20. The nondual voyager *must* have had the experience of the existence of being a "free ego" in the realm of desire.

21. This means that the voyager is no longer battling with the ego as if the ego or the

---

* *Volition-desire* is a state of consciousness found in Impersonal Movement 1. At this point the practitioner of this discipline, having practiced several other stages, experiences what the personal ego is like as it relinquishes center stage, yet still exists. It is at this point that that the student practices bringing the concept of *will* back into the picture and action, but a will that is not personally-owned. To quote from a portion of the IM1 Manual: *This volition-desire is the freedom to decide which movements to actualize and make, as opposed to only receiving the movements and momentum from the plenum. Volition-desire however, is utterly transformed from a "will" activity in the ordinary sense, in that it no longer belongs to anyone but appears in the form of pure choice, unimpeded by fear or greed for gain. The exercise of this volition-desire is joyful: it feels like a child playing . . . but not playacting. It is fully experienced and held, yet it is not captivated by the ego: the sense of proprietorship is largely abated.*

ego's desires were enemies or things that needed to be overcome or vanquished.

22. A free ego is one that is allowed to return to its true function and even allowed to exist in its non-healed form—but with the awareness of its owner (within this framework), who has "put the ego on the table" as a *feature* of the *continuity*.

23. In that state, though we haven't described it in this way before, the practitioner has the ability or power to create nondual or spiritual objects, which is to say, objects imbued with *agency, the ability to alter someone's relationship with their own self and the world around them, and even the ability to make pathways of connection where there were none before.*

   Creating spiritual objects

24. This is a form of power, but not a personal one. If you can, imagine having a relationship with power that does not belong to you: such a relationship does not bring up pride of ownership so much as a sense of responsibility, gratefulness that you can help someone, and compassion for the lot of humanity.

25. These spiritual objects are not emblems of emotions. They are not symbolic of anything other than themselves. Yet, because they are simply themselves, with no extra adornment or manufactured importance, they are potent points of connection with the universal, transcendent or impersonal perspectives of being.

26. They can then become *personally useful* to the expression of the transcendent we call

"the personal," that wave within the greater wave of the world.

27. A chair is an action. Even if no one is sitting in it at any given moment, the chair is not only an action waiting to happen (when someone actually sits in it) but is an object filled with potential, a relationship waiting to happen. It is *already in relationship* to the world just as it is.

28. This is true because, for the voyager, opposites do not have to be united or synthesized in order to reach a transcendent understanding. Instead, *each feature in and of itself can exist in its native form, which is to say, can exist as a complete whole as itself since it is a complete partner not only to every other feature in the world, but* is *the continuity itself*.

29. Put another way, integration of opposites is not necessary in this setting for the voyager to find a way to help themselves and their client to wholeness.

30. The unity of opposites is not our goal. Rather, the goal is to see the whole as it exists in every piece.

31. *Every feature is a portal.* Which is to say, every *feature* in the world can be a healing presence, the apprehension or effect of which can be a resonant return to wholeness for both the client and the voyager.

32. This is a very dynamic condition and the voyager *must* actually be in a nondual

consciousness for this to be a completely positive approach.

33. All the *features* of the world can all be said to exist in the same moment, in the same time, some very vivid or *dense*, some less so. This vast *web* of *features*, interrelating and interconnected, can be in relationship to each other in several ways.

34. One form of connection is through narrative: an empty chair on a stage might invite the narrative of "waiting for someone to come and sit in the chair." And from that starting point, the play begins.

35. Narrative is the primary way humans interact. We constantly create narratives about ourselves, other people and the world. Our entire entertainment industry is based on presenting different forms of narratives. This is an extremely powerful tool and invitation for the human psyche to arrange itself around a perspective or viewpoint.

36. But for the voyager, another relational matrix is possible: that of the web-like interactions between living things, each sentient thing, from rock to water to paper to air.

37. In this arrangement, there is little hierarchy *inherent* in one *feature* and opposed to another. Each member of the web is completely alive, though some sit still for eons and others flit around for a passing moment.

38. We could call this type of organization, with its impact on time and space and especially on the work the voyager has to do, *structural causality*.

39. As I mentioned, in typical, linear causality, the chair is the starting-point for a story, a narrative:

    Who made the chair? Who placed it there? Is it a good-looking chair, well-made and ready to sit on? Who are we waiting for and when will they come? Or, if we are not waiting for anyone, then what feeling are we supposed to have about this single, lonely chair in this room?

40. *Structural causality* on the other hand, is not linear but is dependent upon the actual interrelationships that seem to take place all at once, as if time were condensed to a single moment, a single point.

    IYI: Structural causality is matrix-like. If you can, imagine what time is like in a honeycomb setting, a matrix of all-at-one-ment with different parts of time in each honeycomb cell; this might give you a sense of both time-specific and a-temporal time, both sharing the here and now.

41. A narrative takes place in time. Structural causality is both in time and a-temporal, a line *and* a point.

42. The room, the chair, the person—missing or not—the workmanship, the temperature of the room, in short, anything you can think of, is in a state of constant touching with everything else. This is both a-temporal, as in "time does not apply," and completely temporal, because even the passing of each moment is part of the everything of that moment.

43. We might say without too much grandiosity, that the "universe of sitting" revolves around this chair. The chair is an

opportunity. It is a poetic center around which all the harmonies and motifs of "sitting down" gravitate.

44. The history of the human world is in that chair, from how we noticed that wood would be good for building things, to the art and craft of making a chair, to the tools that were needed to help make it, to painting it and finishing it, to transporting it, and on and on until the web it makes is spun around the world.

45. So this physical thing, which is expressing itself and nothing else, is in the center of the universe and, as I mentioned before, is a gateway to embodying the *continuity*. Only in this case, since this is not a hierarchical sort of causality, *everything else in the scene is in the center of the world as well.*

46. We might say that in an infinite set, every point in infinity is exactly at the center of the universe—and contains that much importance and demands that much respect.

47. The chair then becomes—and always was—a spiritual object. It includes both the personal *and* the impersonal, the transcendent *and* the comfort of a single person.

48. There is the human element and there is something that emerges that is universal, which arises when something is radically itself and nothing else. When this is so, this item or thing is the gateway to the universe.

IYI:
The spiritual teacher Ram Dass once told the story of visiting his mentally ill brother. His brother thought he was Jesus. Ram Dass said that what concerned him most was that his brother thought he was the *only* Jesus Christ. This sad story aside, to fully engage nondual consciousness, every atom is, naturally enough, at the center of an infinite circle we could call *continuity/density*.

49. Because of this, it has power. It has power because it is nothing but itself.

50. It has power because the voyager who made this object was in this state of consciousness: the voyager has decided that she is herself and nothing else. Grandiosity has fallen away. The self, as it were, has begun to fall away, to no longer be the object of adoration.

51. What does a spiritual object look like? Well, its beauty does not reside in its art since it *is* art and not something art was "applied to."

52. It is not sentimental. Sentiment is a symbolic gesture that stands in for real power. It says, essentially, here is my memory of power.

53. This spiritual object then, can look like anything. To eyes that are not in spiritual focus, this power can be missed since it might look like a dull brown stone with no markings. It might be a handful of crushed leaves. It also might be striking and beautiful: the feather of wonderful bird or a piece of polished wood.

> For me, the wonderfully-made French drinking glasses from Duralex are spiritual objects. No kidding!

54. In other words, what it looks like is unimportant. What it *is* is what is important, and it is this *is-ness* itself–with no symbolic overlay–that has the power to help the client remember some truth or activate some missed moment of time or healing.

55. Going further, just for a moment, this object does not even have to exist on the physical plane: it can be a mental image transmitted from this unified place.

56. *Transmission* is an entirely different event than explaining (for instance if you are a teacher) or showing (if you are an artist or dancer or some such).

57. It is how water becomes *holy water*.

58. This activity of *transmission* needs another paradigm beyond the scientific to explain its power. After all, there is nothing in the water itself, nothing extra that makes it holy. The water is not "charged" with some special frequency . . . and yet, it is.

59. The scientific point of view—an extremely useful and powerful vision, but one that has its own limitations—could only explain this by falling back upon the paradigm of *subject and object* and its sister, real or not-real.

60. In this case, this worldview would say that the holiness *resides purely in the mind of the person, their inner psychology, and so on.* That it had *no* objective reality.

61. From this point of view, this would be true.

62. But we always get the answers that a particular filter gives us. The scientific method, which prides itself on "objectivity" and "reproducibility," is actually trapped in some ways since reality is neither exclusively objective or subjective.

63. Science looks for an "objective" answer and there is none. We must go further.

64. While the *method* of making a snowflake *is* reproducible and therefore objective, any individual snowflake is not. Why are there individuals? Why does the universe make

individuals, whether snowflakes or people, over and over again? We may find a temporary answer in evolution and genetic diversity for people. But for galaxies? For universes?

65. Is there some force in the universe (chaos; indeterminacy) that "wants" and "desires" the creation of *individual things*, unique things? Yet the voyager knows from their body outward that *continuity* wants *density* and *density* wants *continuity*.

66. This is of course putting this deep truth in human form and human language, but I am simply trying to give the feeling of this great, impersonal desire.

67. (From an objective-*only* viewpoint, this is a projection of human values and feelings on an objective process, but the nondual view asks further why chaos and indeterminacy lead inextricably to individuality—*and* what the purpose of individuality is.)

68. Simply naming something may capture it under the flag of usefulness, but it does not reveal its heart, its innate intelligence, its reason for being and, I might add, the tenderness (not a scientific term!) with which the universe holds this quality of being and what its usefulness is in the totality of things.

69. The voyager is not after a simple, replicable course of study. The voyager is looking to be entangled with the world and to help their client become re-entangled with the world, since that is where the healing lies, in the natural course of events.

70. My aim in creating Nondual Kabbalistic Healing* (NKH) came from the same desire: it was to create a system that, if someone carefully and bravely followed it, would result in an awakening of spirit with the idea of healing as its central theme.

    The actual procedures the voyager uses to heal, such as, *place your hands in this way, keep this image in mind* and so on, are much less important here. As the healer evolves to nondual consciousness, the techniques become subordinate to the fact that the healer has entered the nondual, creative matrix—in which the choices of how to heal are infinite.

71. And although the Diagnostic Process† uses ambiguity, confusion, clarity, transference and other facets of the totality of our being to arrive at the right healing, it does not set up a settlement in dreamtime—with its emphasis on bucolic mind, imagery, opposites as themselves, gazing, and other disciplines exclusive to voyaging—as the work of the nondual shaman does.

72. Underneath this carefully structured project of NKH was a poem, a poem about our humanity, which cannot be captured or named, not because we have not yet figured out the right name or the right trap, but because it is the moving, uncapturable nature of life itself.

---

* Nondual Kabbalistic Healing® is a healing modality I created that combines my insights into the Jewish mystical tradition of Kabbalah and my studies of Buddhism. It is a transformative, nondual approach that helps heal the healer as well as the client. It is taught at A Society of Souls as a four-year intensive program. You can find more information at: www.societyofsouls.com.
† The Diagnostic Process is part of Nondual Kabbalistic Healing. It is not a characterological approach, but an art form that creates both intimacy and specificity in a session as the healer decides upon the best approach to working with their client.

73. Einstein, until the end of his life, could not reconcile his love of the orderliness of the universe with newer paradigms that showed a kind of indeterminacy at the heart of creation.

74. To my mind this was not a failure of Einstein's intellect but of his artistic ability: this indeterminacy at the heart of nature is not disorderly: it is an orderliness of a different and perhaps higher level.

75. From my point of view, I expect this dance—between pure orderliness and the version of orderliness that shows its indeterminate face first—to go on forever, as first *numeric space* and then *linguistic space* come to the forefront to be noticed. In other words, *continuity* and *density* are in constant motion, touching, being touched, wave-like and point-like, completely interrelated and simultaneously completely separate, glowing, self-illuminated in every state that turns its face toward us.

76. In our own separate-*only* state, we might have trouble understanding that all these opposite sounding descriptions are a single thing.

77. But as we know from our spiritual practice, which does not have this prejudice baked into it, what the mind has trouble with, the heart can easily see.

78. So we could say that what we are after as nondual voyagers is a work that is *reliably non-duplicable*, that is, matchless and inimitable.

79. Simultaneously, the whole project of this book is to set out a number of rungs on the ladder so that each person can climb it, find a footing, and thereby find their own unique way.

80. We no longer seek to arrive at the "right healing" as a matter of some prior aim. There is no path but the one that we are walking, as trusted guides who are, at the same time, guiding ourselves and the ones we work with.

81. In other words, our creations—whether they are nondual healings, voyages or spiritual objects—are unique and alive . . . and we can do or make them over and over again, each one not captured by our echoing mind, but free *with* our desire and volition. We do not need to become empty to voyage: we can also be full.

82. As nondual voyagers and healers working for someone else, within the world of our *turn*, we can ask for—and receive—these transmittable gifts for our clients.

83. These spiritual objects, which is to say, objects that are only and just themselves and yet exist as relational nexuses, as entangling and relational places, are imbued with power that does not reside in the subject/object world.

84. They cannot be second-hand, which is to say, received from someone else.

85. They cannot be manufactured artificially. They cannot be faked. They cannot be a feather or stone or crystal or mantra or

ritual that has not been arrived at through the circuitous route of the voyager's descent to the truth of his or her being.

86. They cannot be built up from neurosis, wherein the voyager is solving some inner problem of self-worth or of having been unloved in an earlier existence.

87. It is through the voyager's descent into the real that any of these objects *gain* any power.

88. Whether it is something written or painted, carved on stone, a stone itself, an activity to do, something to act out, a beverage to drink and so on, we are going directly to the place the old shamans went to by using drugs—without the drugs.

89. The drugs were only doorways into seeing a non-egoic reality.

> "Non-egoic reality" does not mean "without an ego." It means "*with* the ego as something—as a *density itself*—that is 'on the table.'"

90. Our job is somewhat harder, since we are *including the ego in our worldview, in our Wholeness*. We are not transient visitors to some version of an interconnected world that is devoid of the *densities* of our own egos. Every *thing* is included.

91. This is a rough-and-tumble business.

92. What we bring to our client is potent because it does not encourage or condone further splitting. It refuses to bow to some abstract idea of what a person should or should not be but includes it all—even resistance and splitting itself. Doing this, this "non-doing" that is so hard to achieve, sets the Great Healing in motion.

93. Some we can heal, others we cannot, but denial of the fact that our lives are a type of wholeness that is made up of pieces does no good.

94. All the healing the nondual voyager wants to do starts and ends with awakening to the truth of things as they actually are.

Returning to the Source of Power

1. The voyager needs to be a center of power in order to do his or her work as a healer from the unitive state.

2. But as I mentioned before, we need to reassess our ideas of what power actually is and is not.

3. When we are neurotic, or more correctly, when we still do not know the specifics and origins of our neuroses and are still mostly mastered by our distortions of being and doing because they are still largely unconscious, we do not have power in the way a nondual voyager must have it.

4. When we are still unconsciously in thrall to the past, with its wounds and misconceptions, its generalizations and unexpressed hurts, we do not have power.

5. It is important to add the caveat that we are not talking about any sort of perfection here, or of "being beyond" our neuroses. Instead, we are talking about the level of awareness and honesty the healer has about their own state of being.

6. Our power to communicate with the subtleties of reality is based on our level of personal honesty matched with our skill.

7. So a voyager's power stands on a foundation of *gnosis* or knowledge and, in this case, the understanding of the origins of his or her suffering.

8. *Gnosis* of this sort automatically brings with it humility and a softening of our egoic boundaries and self-concern. It does so as we intimately know our imperfections and practice kindness and acceptance toward all of them.

9. Part of this kindness can exist because we begin to deeply understand and admit our inability to completely conquer our imperfections or even change them substantially. We come to understand that these imperfections were born of saving our lives in the best way we (then) knew how to do so.

10. This is a kindness that takes into account the challenge of incarnation *and* environment. It is clear-eyed about the human condition—even as we continue to try to improve and be better people, better companions and better healers.

11. As, and when, we know this, we no longer feel as defensive about who we are.

12. Although the ego-self is always making sure it can survive the next moment, its "workload" is greatly diminished, as we no longer have to defend against the threat of non-existence or annihilation we feared would come to pass if we revealed who we truly were, warts and all, helplessness and all.

13. Our admission of this ultimate powerlessness is what our power—now no longer only personal—is paradoxically built on.

14. Our admission and acceptance of powerlessness makes us like everyone else.

15. We lose our "special position" and show up as others do, as beings caught in a world we did not make, did not invite ourselves into, hoping to stay as long as possible in this life, and fearing leaving the very things that cause us pain.

16. This joining with others—while destroying the specialness we counted on to protect ourselves from life, also reveals our true specialness and allows our uniqueness to shine through.

17. We could even say that as our "decorated self" diminishes, the unadorned self that loves life and healing in its unique way and style comes to the forefront.

18. This practice of pursuing *gnosis* is a major cornerstone in the voyager's training.

19. Likewise, the practice of *noticing life,* rather than simply living it without introspection, is a cornerstone of our practice.

20. Life constantly presents us with opposites: things we like and things we do not like.

21. If you meditate on this for a moment, you will see that this statement alone accounts for much of the dissatisfactions we often feel about our lives, other people's lives, and the world in general.

22. This is a powerless condition.

23. To attain real power—including the power to change the things we do not like—we

must learn to take into our selves, into our bodies and consciousness, the dissonance created by these opposites of life, not singly, clinging first to one and then running from the other, or even finding strategies that help us cling to our desired pole more effectively, but as simultaneous, mutually-arising conditions that *cannot ever be separated, especially if we are seeking to see the center of creation.*

24. Please note that this is not a contradiction of what I have said before: the nondual voyager lives in the dynamic world populated by the self-illuminated *features* that make up the *continuity. Simultaneously,* in order to be able to live in this marketplace of "things-exactly-as-they-are," the voyager must have experienced the spaciousness that comes from having been able to hold these opposites and feel the quality or unity that arises when their united presence gives way to a state that includes them and yet goes beyond them into something we have called in other settings, "the third thing."

25. A good example of this is the MAGI Process, which at its heart is a shamanistic and voyaging practice. In this Process, each Step exists perfectly as itself, its message dynamic and shimmering and holographic. At the same time, *all of the Steps* unite into a vision of reality that is the *continuity/density* itself.

26. Self-improvement is a powerful motive force in every person's desire to go on a spiritual path. It is something that lives in the personal sphere and something we cannot dispense with as long as we are alive. Yet,

the culmination of all of this improvement is to live in the perfection of all of this imperfection and improvement. The spiritual path always—eventually—lands us right back here. Having gone on a long journey of attaining knowledge, we give it up to simply live and help. With what? Our knowledge of course!

27. This is simply another of the opposites of life, brought into high relief by the spiritual path itself. Power arises as we make this journey only to stop this journey. Then voyaging begins, the journey that goes nowhere and everywhere in the same moment.

28. The voyager who has power has learned that life is choice because they have unlocked many of the chains of the past that prohibited choice. Again, at the same time, the voyager realizes how little choice there really is in the totality of being and finds freedom in the chains of being alive. The opposites of life keep recurring.

29. There is "day" because there is "night." There is "life" because there is "death." Illness? Because there is health . . . Ego because there is the non-egoic. The relative world because there is the absolute. And so on.

30. When we are still psychologically striving to attain all that we could not attain as children, to redress our wounds and conquer our fears, living in the "now" solely for the purpose of righting the wrongs of the past, we cannot hold these opposites without unconsciously deadening ourselves,

keeping a "stiff upper lip," and in other words, submerging the wounds in the hope of something better. True choice has not yet arrived.

31. Trying to choose one pole over the other will not—ever—put us in touch with the kind of power I am talking about.

32. The power I am talking about is nondual: it is not a power *in reaction* to something else or toward something else but is something that automatically springs to our awareness as we have healed enough of our personal pain to bear the increased energy brought by both the union of opposites *and* the allowing of opposites to exist in their native state.

33. This union and acceptance of opposites cannot be accomplished without deep insight into our wounds, their origin, and how they affect our behavior in the present moment. Only then can things "be exactly as they are"—the spiritual prerequisite to real change.

34. We must also attempt and express effort to improve ourselves. This part of the voyage is not about simply accepting without effort every state we are in.

35. When we have explored the origins of our suffering in the personal world, no longer trying to escape to the altitudes of dissociative joy, we have increased the width of our foundation; our bandwidth has increased and broadened. Because of this, we have the capability to stand in the flux of opposites as they are, unafraid of our

human sorrows, meeting them directly, and finding a kind of joy that has no opposites because it was born of the union of these two worlds and not our oscillation between them.

36. So our power comes from the union of limitation and freedom, from the union of sorrow and joy, from the conscious understanding of the role our imperfections play in our lives, which is actually one of guide, key-holder and alchemist who turns lead into gold through the power of *awakening kindness*.

37. Being aware of opposites both as facets of a third state of wholeness and as "things-in-themselves," which is where the voyager ultimately lives, is what allows kindness to sprout in our hearts, to take root in our body and blossom.

38. To find this kindness as a real and living quality, we must walk directly into our suffering, toward some of the things that made us as we are.

39. Every human being is made to confront—by the very set-up of incarnation—an imperfect set of parents and their own, undiscovered and unconscious imperfections as well.

40. We term this moment *poisoned ground* because that phrase captures the dilemma each of us has to face, that of needing to take in the nourishment of our environment *even as it poisons us*.

    Poisoned and Poisoning Ground

41. As Samuel Beckett says,

> *Enormous prison, like a hundred thousand cathedrals. Never anything else any more, from this time forth. And in it, somewhere, perhaps—riveted, tiny—the prisoner. How can he be found? [. . . .]*
>
> *I can't go on. I'll go on.**

42. This is the dilemma each of us finds ourselves in from the moment we are born.

43. Here is an extended excerpt from one of my journals describing this dangerous territory:

    > *Because the transaction between parent and child is damaged by the unavoidable imperfections and unconsciousness of the parent and other parts of the environment, the ego, which is both reflected in the world and reflects the world, does not work properly.*
    >
    > *The ego needs a balance between allowing internal conditions to manifest and having the world/parent mirror the rightness of the ego's essential existence, even if it is sometimes too much of one thing or another.*
    >
    > *Faced with this disruption of healthy processes, the ego—which is a divine creation, and one specializing in both separate existence and in the inner desire to return to Oneness—constantly tries to make oneness by whatever means it has available to itself.*
    >
    > *It is a oneness-making machine and continues running on whatever fuel it can find.*

---

* Samuel Beckett, *The Unnamable*, Grove Press, 1978.

Not having a truly healthy outer partner (the parent) in this process, it uses various forms of self-reflection to make up the deficit. It also takes second-hand versions of itself as the real thing and tries to incorporate them in the equation of being a person.

It is a cut-and-paste job that is always in danger of falling apart.

Remember: it does this because there is an inner movement toward wholeness and health. The ego always moves ahead, trying to find Wholeness.

We become objects in the drama of our lives, acting out a story in the world instead of a life.

This is like a mirror looking at itself: In order for this to be possible, the mirror must first be in fragments.

This is what happens to us. We end up in a form of isolated aloneness, looking at ourselves looking, an infinite regress of mirrors, in a state of trance about the true nature of the world and our self.

We are pointed the wrong way.

Individuals who objectify themselves in this way cannot have empathy for the very self they are determined to see as the center of the universe. Their self is a constructed thing, a mechanism rather than a living creature, and sensing that, this self always falls short, even as they try to pretend it is in fine shape.

A healthy relationship with the Self is neither subjective nor objective exclusively. It is sometimes not even noticed.

Therefore, the self that we think of objectively is not the Real Self, but a thing, a creation of extreme fear, the fear we feel when we have been forced to fracture in order to survive, when we are forced to incorporate the other in order to continue to be "whole."

Because we have no real relationship with the self in this state, the self is seen only in the light of comparison, through which it is always in danger of being maligned, swamped, and denigrated.

It never really measures up.

In a sense we could say that the self, which should have a certain type of balance between in- and out-flow of consciousness, is out of balance from both ends. In a healthy state, we have inner yearnings, an inner sense of self, a feeling of place we can rely on to know who we are. We are also open to influences and feedback from the world and others.

In-flowing and out-flowing get confused, and we use one for the other.

Our inner self should flow outward to the world, telling the world who we are. Instead, this inner self flowing out is always asking a question: "Who should I be to feel safe? To have you think well of me?"

And instead of the world coming in to the inner self as a form of pleasure or communication, it comes in as a constant threat: are we good enough? Are we supported enough? Can we survive?

44. The understanding of poisoned ground, and the hard work that is necessary to heal

it, is the beginning of the foundation of power because it will lead us to the *is-ness* of the world, the simultaneity of the *continuity/density*.

45. Going on this part of the journey, the healing ego, now no longer quite as focused on trying to turn a sow's ear into silk, begins to concentrate on the self *as it is*.

    > Self-improvement = seeing things as they are.

46. Energies once disrupted are now returned to the self for non-neurotic expression.

47. But the task of knowing and healing must go further. What follows is the complete text of the next step in this process, which I call "The Active Side of Poisoning Ground."

48. The work of "The Active Side of Poisoning Ground" becomes most useful to the extent that we have familiarity with our own *poisoned ground*, which is to say, the elements of our upbringing in which our own soul was used to make someone else, rather than ourselves, whole.

49. It was created by Arlene Shulman and myself as advanced work for our healing students. It describes how the poisoned ground is kept alive and active by the act of passing on our poisoned ground to others.

50. We do this not because we are evil, but because our unhealed egos are terrified of seeing and feeling the suffering that lies beneath our conscious minds and which is expressed in the dilemma of poisoned ground. We do not yet understand that feeling the suffering of our poisoned ground is the only way to heal it.

51. By passing it on to others, we are participating in a conspiracy to keep our suffering hidden from ourselves, a conspiracy orchestrated by our un-integrated egos and their limited vision of what will ultimately keep us safe.

52. The voyager, on the other hand, takes a different route, does not seek to sublimate this suffering in some abstract knowledge of "God" or "Reality" or "Oneness," or mysticisms of any sort. Instead, they choose to walk directly, slowly, into the state of things as they are, knowing somehow, deep inside, that freedom and the ability to help, the ability to break the chain of *poisoning ground* and bring healing where it is needed, comes from walking into fears, real and imagined, only to come out whole, perhaps for the first time.

> This is an outgrowth of the voyager's acknowledgment of a *single world* and all that it contains.

The Active Side of Poisoning Ground

Men are admitted into Heaven not because they have curbed and governed their passions or have no passions, but because they have cultivated their understandings. The treasures of Heaven are not negations of passion, but realities of intellect, from which all the passions emanate uncurbed in their eternal glory. The fool shall not enter into Heaven let him be ever so holy.
  – William Blake

To become a healing presence, we need to make peace with ourselves. This is done through non-attachment. But what does non-attachment mean? It is not purification: it is no longer being ordered around by our smallest parts. We learn to do this not by the "moral road" but by the path of actualization.
  – Jason Shulman

The cure—or the healing—of the poisoned ground aspect of our being is threatening to the unhealed aspects of our egos—at the very same time as this injured part of us longs to return to wholeness and exist as a vibrant part of life.

One of the ways we determinedly, though unconsciously, keep the foundational suffering of our existential dilemma hidden from ourselves—in a misguided effort to reduce our pain and lack of authenticity—is by passing on our suffering to others without taking an introspective look at it first. By doing this, we essentially make others carry our pain for us, leaving us free to deny its existence in ourselves.

For this aspect of working without suffering, we need to engage with a more muscular approach. While belief in, and understanding of, our thoughts and feelings was very important from a psychological point of view (in order to trace and heal our historical wounds), now we will call into question the way in which we automatically believe in our thoughts and feelings and act on them as if they were a true picture of the world and not a system in and of themselves. Systems can be changed once we notice the pattern and challenge its habitual gravity.

While this exploration is not limited to negative thoughts only, we will examine these so-called negative thoughts and feelings and the behaviors that result from believing and acting upon them. We start here because these so-called negative feelings/thoughts seem to be so much more plentiful and certainly much more seductive. We seem to always be ready to believe the worst thoughts we have about ourselves.

To do this, we will revisit the poisoned ground from a new perspective that we will call "the poisoning ground." As I mentioned above, *poisoning ground* is yet another strategy we believe—falsely—will protect us from the suffering of becoming aware of our *poisoned* ground.

In our discussions about the poisoned ground—so called because this metaphor highlights our impossible predicament in which the essential relational nourishment of life is simultaneously toxic, misleading, and anti-life—we have concentrated on how the parent's unconscious, unexpressed and unexplored pain is transmitted to the child. The child is placed in the position of having to save the parent in order to save their own lives, at exactly the same developmental time as the child needs to be supported and cherished for who they are, exactly *as they are*. This is the same dilemma the parents unsuccessfully negotiated for themselves in their own development. We are only set free by feeling this pain, this loneliness, and this inauthenticity, in their original states. In dealing with the poisoned ground we learn to deal with its effects upon *ourselves* as perpetrated by *others*.

We have not however, talked about how this poison is sustained, protected and even nurtured during our life so that we, like carriers of an emotional plague (to use Wilhelm Reich's phrase), pass it on to others as a way of trying to protect ourselves from its impact upon our body, mind and spirit.

THE ACTIVE SIDE OF POISONING GROUND

First we need to understand *why* we would pass this poison on.

The most direct answer is: we act in ways we believe will help us survive the impact of the poisoning we ourselves suffered.

Within the arena of the poisoning ground, we actively pursue a path we hope will keep us safe from the effects of the poisoned ground visited upon us by our parents. But in actuality, this instinctive agenda only serves to pass along these early wounds in their entirety—while simultaneously keeping us in the trance foisted upon us in the first place. In other words, our attempt at a cure is also our way of sinking deeper into the problem we are trying to avoid. We institutionalize our poisoned ground and carry it forward into the present moment, both hiding it from our consciousness and simultaneously giving it new life.

We are emotionally poisoned because something is expected of us that is impossible to give: we are asked to become the healthy soul for our parent, to solve our parent's anxieties, sorrows and loneliness by our very being, through how we move, behave, touch, act, think and feel. Thus we exchange *our* soul—the soul we are born to find, nourish and develop—for our parent's own need. They in turn, abandon their true job as parents (caring for our soul) in order to seek solace in us. In this way *inside* and *outside* get confused. In a healthy situation, we are supposed to discover our own soul *inside* of ourselves. The *outside* world—in the form of our parents, schools, and other people—are supposed to mirror our development, guide it, and correct it *in the cause of our own self*.

Now, however, our soul's development and authenticity seem to be *outside*, and we learn to look *there*, to our parents and cues from the world, to see how *we are doing*, to see if we are ok. Our reality now comes from the outside. Similarly, the soul-seeking parent looks to the outside (us) for what should be found within. Everything is backwards.

Learning about this imperfect journey is the work of the psychological part of our journey as spiritual beings: we learn the outer story and the inner story; we learn eventually to go our own way more and more. This begins the healing process. However, the healing cannot be complete within the psychological paradigm. To complete our healing, or at least to deepen it, we must go to the nondual perspective and, in so doing, abandon the very things that brought us to the very precipice of health itself.

The psychological work focuses on the interface between the person (ourselves) and their environment (the world, other people, our family, etc.), between personal history and the objective world. Through this work we illuminate the story of our lives.

The tools we use in this pursuit are: understanding, meaning, enlightenment, awakening, God, human certainty, the certainty of un-certainty and so on. It is a noble endeavor carried forward by psychotherapy and by aspects of many spiritual paths. This is how we can get deep psychological insight, which as we know, is healing, freeing and essential.

This work is never done, but at a certain point, the context can change to a level that is more integrated, which in ASOS we term *briatic*. Briatic—which name from the Kabbalistic universe of *Briah*, here is used as an equivalent to "nondual." Briah *contains* the psychological universe, so psychological work is never lost but continues in a more integrated form, which requires us to go even more deeply on our journey to real freedom.

Briatic or nondual work only becomes a possibility as we do our psychological work. This work relaxes some of our vigilance so that the call from the nondual perspective begins to be heard. We might say that some egoic stability and a newly developed sense of trust in life are essential precursors to beginning the briatic adventure.

Now we are less interested in the information of our history—which we have already deeply explored—and become more interested in "something else," which at first we have a hard time describing. We become less interested in "he said/she said" and the perspectives of who wounded whom and how, and begin to wonder what wholeness might be like, a wholeness that might still have all of this suffering but be somehow beyond it, a wholeness that is not so much about seeking as receiving the already-present bounty of a lit-up universe.

This new level of work requires—above all things—the return *of all energies to their proper places. All things in one place at one time. Inside must return to inside and outside to outside. This is how power—always in its benign form—arises from the is-ness or thus-ness of all things, which is, in actuality, their natural state. This takes will and effort.*

An example of this is what we call "riding the wave of transference" which is what we call this method of returning energy to its source. Transference, in a psychological sense, is traditionally understood to be the projection of feelings from past relationships or events onto other people or events in the present moment. It is not an example of "being in the now," but of imposing a vision of the past on the present moment. Most often this diversion of feelings and beliefs is unconscious and is a way of automatically replaying or carrying over trauma from the past—often in an unconscious attempt to replay it, hoping in vain for another outcome. As such, transference is looked at pathologically as the way the unconscious expresses its feelings when these feelings are not in the conscious mind.

In the work of Nondual Kabbalistic Healing, however, we are most interested in the fact of the *existence of transference itself* and how meeting transference in the moment in a new and fresh way actually opens the doors of perception *for the healer* or, in this case, the nondual voyager, allowing them to perceive ever more deeply things that might not even be connected to the object of the transference itself.

How is it possible that this instantaneous communication goes on? From the pathological view, transference seems to be the unjustified projection of internal, mostly historical feelings onto someone else. But from our point of view, this "reaching out" is part of the sensorium of every human and goes on all the time in our daily lives. And, like our other senses, transference is one of the ways we know reality. It is also fallible of course—but so are our ears and eyes and other senses. Finally, to re-state perhaps the most important point, riding the wave of transference is something the healer or voyager does for themselves in order to create intimacy—with both their own self and the person they are working with. Because of this, we approach transference not so much from a psychological point of view, seeking to discern additional information about the person's background and neuroses, but almost *physically*, as an object within our sensorium we need to relate to *without changing it in any way*. The ability to do this takes practice and, to continue the physical metaphor, the building up of the body that has a broad enough "bandwidth" to feel the transferences—their own and the client's—without judgment or shattering.

So the voyager, in the same way as the nondual kabbalistic healer, looks at transference not so much as a problem but as a question. The question turns out to be, underneath, the same in every case: *How can I be happy? How can I be whole? Where do you fit into my picture of who I am?*

From a completely unconscious point of view, which is where transference usually arises from, transference seems to be an event or condition on the outside that affects the person on the inside. Unconsciously, the person "uses" the world to act out the inner drama they are trying to understand or work through.

But when the healer allows themselves to feel the transferential energy vividly and not defend against it or, more precisely and completely, allows *even their own counter-transference to consciously exist* as yet another "thing" in the mandala of this interaction, they in essence place transference back to its actual origin, as an inner psychic event. Then the energy of the transference is placed back where it belongs and accrues to the opening of new levels of consciousness in the healer, eventually leading to understanding or an awakening of continued self-realization.

This hard-won higher level of consciousness begins to show us the existence and impact of poisoned ground on our lives. Then, as we begin to be consciously aware of our poisoned ground and, moving onward, seek to understand the dynamics of the active *poisoning* ground, we must begin to call into question some of the very tools that helped us become aware of these formerly hidden dynamics: thinking and feeling. Thinking and feeling were for a long time sacrosanct. In fact, we used these tools to help us realize more of our nature and to free us from historical pain.

But now, even these "holy-of-holies," these faculties we worked so hard to mature and use as tools for our own liberation, must be called into question or seen in a new, more helpful, light. These faculties don't disappear—we remain able to think and feel—but are seen freshly as elements revealed within a bigger territory, which is not a territory that thinking and feeling can discern.

This insight allows us to drop to a new level of understanding, a level unhindered by the myopic focus on thinking and feeling as if they were the only arbiter and path to truth. Now, thinking and feeling are no longer seen just as tools to find truth but also as the *materials* of which the poison ground was made, first by our parents' thoughts and feelings, and then by our own.

In the ways I will enumerate below, we can begin to illuminate exactly how the poisoned ground was transmitted to us and how we inadvertently transmit it to others and, in this way, keep it alive.

When we understand this circuit of the further transmission of the poisoning ground, we not only protect other people from catching this plague of miseducation but complete our own healing as well. Now we are at the deepest level of relationship as a conscious activity in the present moment. This present moment still *contains* all the elements of suffering that took place in the past but now we are no longer under its thrall, no longer asleep in our effort to avoid feeling this suffering, but awake. Now, curing the self and curing others happens in the same moment as we are no longer separated from the world. It happens in one place, at one time, not through thought or understanding but through action and nourishment.

The current of this transmission of the pain we borrowed from our parents and made our own is perpetuated and institutionalized by our unexamined adherence to an inner "religion" we don't even know we are practicing:

1. the practice of believing our thoughts are real things;

2. acting on our thoughts as if they were real and truthful;

3. the practice of believing our feelings;

4. the practice of acting on our feelings . . . as if they are real.

The poisoned ground seeks to perpetuate itself by having the world do the job the inner self should be doing and the inner self do the work the world must do—a mirror of what we were asked to do as children when our parents sought to use us to ease their own unexamined pain instead of supporting our true autonomy. Because the psychological tension in the wounded one (all of us!) is too much to bear, the one wounded in this way seeks to have the world—that is other people—correct the imbalance, negate the feeling, hold or erase the tension. We can notice this when we find ourselves irritated with other people for "not doing something," though the doing—if we look at it carefully—is irrational. In other words, we seek to have other people's behavior heal the emptiness and tension we find in ourselves. An example: The other day in a coffee shop I had to squeeze around a father and son who were standing directly in front of the trash. As I bent around the teenage son—who had been simply chatting with his dad, both of them pausing in front of the trash as they talked, I heard the dad say *Why were you standing there?* to his son. In fact, both the father and son were blocking the area that led to the trash, absorbed in chatting. I watched the young man instantly lose himself for a moment, become somewhat bewildered and shamed and then come back to equilibrium as the transaction of passing the father's poisoned ground to the son was completed.

The only true resolution is to return to the subjective self, bringing the energy back to its starting point. In the above example, the father might have caught *his own* shame and humiliation, passed on to him by one of *his* parents, and borne the suffering of that ancient wound himself without passing it on to his son. This "bearing our own suffering" is the essential tool for achieving nondual awareness. It is a form of true spiritual alchemy, which sets the stage for the return of the totality of our being and our true wholeness.

This causes a great deal of suffering at first as formerly and perhaps still-unbearable pain is held in consciousness, but the wounded one must be willing to undergo this suffering in the name of further spiritual enlightenment. We begin this by practicing *satyagraha*.

Definition:

Civil disobedience and non-cooperation as practiced under satyagraha are based on the "law of suffering," a doctrine that the endurance of suffering is a means to an end. This end usually implies a moral upliftment or progress of an individual or society. Therefore, non-cooperation in satyagraha is in fact a means to secure the cooperation of the opponent consistently with truth and justice. (Wikipedia)

In other words, *satyagraha* is not simple resistance: it is resolute and unwavering; it is focused *relationship*.

The relationship we must continue here is between ourselves and the unbearable feelings of defeat, annihilation, objectification, loneliness and all the other injuries, the avoidance of which started us on this journey in the first place. We give up, in essence, trying to have the world heal us, and instead return to ourselves to begin the process of healing. When we do this, we cease transmitting this pain.

In other words, *though we have these thoughts and feelings within ourselves, and feel compelled to eliminate them through the pseudo-solution of having the world ("other people") take them away, through hard effort we extricate ourselves from unerringly believing our thoughts and feelings as objective reporters of some external reality and instead begin to see them as part of a system that interprets and even constructs reality.*

Now, instead of acting on all of our thoughts and feelings, instead of being *within the system of thought*, we must take a new look at thoughts and feelings from a more nuanced and distanced point of view, understanding that far from being "objective things," thoughts and feelings are always editorializing about reality. They are not external but spring from a ground that is already colored with unreality. They are a syntax in and of themselves and not "objective tools" for describing what is actually there. In essence, thoughts and feelings *create* what is there the way "hammer-consciousness" sees everything as something to *nail down*.

Unlike a purely psychological approach, we no longer seek to "resolve" these feelings away by understanding and insight. Now we need to work with the raw energies themselves *directly, for the first time.*

However, most of us do not do this. Instead we use a variety of strategies to maintain this intolerable dissatisfaction with ourselves and the world with the irrational hope that it can be solved by re-creating a new "other" who will finally see the light and act in ways that we believe will heal us.

By becoming aware of all these strategies, we can begin to free ourselves from essentially imprisoning effects on ourselves and others.

Some of these strategies are:

- gossiping
- maligning (but usually thought of as simply "talking about what is going on")
- colluding (allowing this type of behavior to go on, seemingly because of peer pressure but really because it serves our own purposes)
- self-doubt (the bad kind, not the good kind!) and other modalities
- blame
- self-righteousness

These strategies, which are supported by our thinking and feeling, are ways of keeping the essential poison at arm's length. The vehicle for accomplishing this is based on believing our thoughts and feelings without question.

Exposing the relationship between our thinking and feeling and the effort to avoid suffering by maintaining illusion is only broken by being willing to take all psychic energies back into ourselves and being willing to suffer. This must be achieved step by step.

- The *first* step is *seeing* the thoughts and feelings (they are so much a part of our behavior that for the most part they are invisible to us.)
- The *second* is seeing our unwavering belief in them as something real.
- The *third* is understanding the difference between psychological understanding—which can bring a degree of freedom—and being entrapped by believing that thinking and feeling are "objective truths" and can be corrected but never questioned as an entire system of navigating reality.

- The *fourth* step is watching the strategies we have developed to keep this system going, which we can list in this way as well:
    - maligning
    - joining with others in a mob mentality
    - blaming other people
    - the right to "earned or righteous anger"
    - holding a grudge
    - complaining . . . et al.

We use these sub-systems to keep ourselves from seeing that ultimately thoughts and feelings are syntax and, being syntax, have profound limitations within them even as they add to our freedom. (We rarely ask the question, *What is reality like when not obscured by our belief in feeling/thought?*)

- The *fifth* step is observing what comes up when we do <u>not</u> readily believe our feelings/thoughts but also seek to stay in relationship with them by not repressing or "disappearing them." (This "disappearing of thoughts and feelings" is one of the mistaken strategies often employed in spiritual work.) You may find that powerful feelings arise in you either emotionally or somatically as you enter this truly non-violent path of non-cooperation.

- The *final* stage is the active, dynamic resistance. In other words, we enter a stage where we engage our positive will, or *kavannah*, to this end. We become willing to endure the suffering we must as we bring the energy displayed in thoughts and feelings back into our own body, putting our body on the line in this way. Now we no longer pass our karma on to others. We willingly disengage from all the interactive strategies we use to alleviate the poisoned ground inside of us—strategies such as maligning and gossip. We become a kind of alchemical furnace, which

> transmutes the poisoned ground into its original primal energy. This is true compassion and freedom.

Most importantly, we need to engage all of this in an atmosphere of self-love and kindness.

The healing of the poisoned ground is the gateway to seeing Reality in its luminescent and true state. Its very existence, therefore, holds great promise—as well as great peril if it is not healed.

To apply all of this to our daily lives, we will be working with *satyagraha,* or true civil disobedience, as it applies to our self-protective thoughts and feelings. Students who take this mission on should follow the five steps outlined above.

Please realize that this work is very challenging but brings great rewards. It could be called "The True Cultivation of Spacious Mind."

This is because we do this practice not for moral reasons, although it will certainly have moral effects, but for the sake of our own freedom. We could say that we no longer want to be slaves to our thoughts and feelings.

The phases of practice for this adventure are described below.

First, practice Phase One (Step One *and* Step Two) for *at least* three weeks. At the end of that time you may begin to practice Phase Two *only* if you feel ready to do so.

If you choose to go on to Phase Two, please allow yourself to weave back and forth between the first two phases.

Engage with Phase Three only when you are sure you are not avoiding relationship with the power of your own suffering.

Phase One

Step One:

Please begin to observe how often and how much of your body and mind are taken up with thoughts and feelings of:

- Judging
- Comparing
- Denigrating
- Doubting
- Self-righteous entitlement and anger
- Blame
- Complaining

Notice that these feelings/thoughts may be directed toward another or yourself. Your first job is simply to be aware, to wake up to how pervasive these feelings/thoughts are. (You may be surprised to find that these types of feelings/thoughts go on fifty to one-hundred—or more!—times a day!)

Chances are good that if you find these feelings/thoughts directed at others during the day, they have already been directed at yourself!

Step Two:

The second step is to recognize them simply as "thoughts" (remember: feelings are a kind of thought at a different level), not necessarily to be believed or seen as real.

Phase Two

Notice the strategies you use to save yourself from feeling the poisoned ground. The strategies are described above in the text of step four: *maligning, colluding, engaging in mob mentality, self-righteous complaining, gossiping, holding grudges and delighting in others' misfortunes (schadenfreude), judging others, severe self-judgment, arguing with others in your head*, and so on.

Without yet *stopping these behaviors*, try to notice what benefits they bring you. For example:

- Filling up emptiness
- Relieving tension
- Making yourself feel safe
- Making yourself feel you belong
- Reducing your helplessness

Also begin to notice how acting in these ways might in reality have the opposite effect: making you feel lonely, small, dishonest, anxious, and more self-judging.

Phase Three

Here we will actually practice *satyagraha*.

For the sake of freedom, we will willingly engage in non-cooperation toward our own behavior. While maintaining awareness of these poisons, we will actually stop colluding, maligning, blaming, acting out of self-righteousness, and gossiping with others.

This includes the very difficult cessation of these behaviors with our spouses and partners.

This is not about repression! It is about setting the stage for an alchemical event. Observe what comes up when you disengage from these activities. Here we are willing to suffer for the sake of liberation. The side effect is that we cease to pass on our karma of suffering.

Observe the changes inside as you begin to return what is *inside* to the *inside* and what is *outside* to the *outside*.

All of this work can only be done in the spirit of deep compassion and self-acceptance!

Expect failure.

What we *do not* want is to use this as another way to judge ourselves. In fact, if self-judgment arises, please see that as just another feeling/thought, another small part of ourselves that we do not need to be ordered around by.

Also: as you get practiced at not acting upon these thoughts and feelings, expect the feelings/thoughts to continually arise. Our job is not to repress them but to recognize them and choose to be free.

Please remember: we are not doing this practice to develop some sort of "purity" in thought and deed. We are doing this practice to be free from the tyranny of our thoughts and compulsions of our feelings.

More on Returning to the Source of Power

1. All of this noble and difficult work serves to *return all of our energies to our own self.*

2. This is the beginning of the arriving at, and having access to, the power the voyager needs to heal his or her own self and the self of others.

3. This is a remarkable moment, one that aligns us with the lineage of others, long gone and yet to come, who have found the inescapable pull of the truth and who have decided—against the advice of their smallest parts—to follow it.

4. But even here, we must go a bit further.

5. From a non-psychological standpoint or, put another way, a directly alchemical one, it is best to turn toward *life as it is* to instruct us further.

6. Because we are "choosing creatures," always trying to find the way to safety, we often

enter and leave many realms during a typical day.

7. Speaking for myself and my own journey, my days are filled with tens of states I pass through from one moment to another.

8. When I am not centered on the overall truth of life, each of these states seems like an endless and final territory that I have somehow found myself trapped in, without my conscious volition or desire.

9. But even in those moments, I can find the nondual choice of how to live within this pendulating world.

10. The question then becomes one of how we can meet the oscillating conditions of our daily lives in a way that increases our nondual relationship with power.

11. Nondual power is power that no one "owns" and which exists in our awareness only as we allow the waves of our temporary individual self to co-arise with the great uninterrupted and waveless sea of being.

12. An example: we are in hell realms at some point every day and, for some of us, even if it is for seconds at a time, many times during a typical day. *Being in hell*

13. (One of our first tasks is to actually *notice* that that is true and to not ignore these momentary, but potent, fluctuations in an effort to avoid having our suffering come to consciousness.)

14. Once we know this to be true, to prepare for a voyage, the traveler—rather than

mitigating or "smoothing out" or even "healing" this hell realm—should consider *allowing it to be hell.* And further, being non-reactive to it.

15. This "non-reactivity" is quite different from the "stiff upper lip" I mentioned before. It comes only from accepting the opposites of life with profound kindness for the very existence of these opposites.

16. Instead, we might see this hell-realm as yet another manifestation or portion of our own nervous system, our karma, and even our liberation. We might understand that all beings go through these realms many times a day, often without the benefit of understanding even a bit about why this occurs—on the personal, psychological level, and on the existential level as well.

17. In this way, we could allow the direct energy of contact with this realm to occur without it being short-circuited into yet another psychological dilemma to be "healed away," or "fixed away."

18. Instead, in the spirit of *satyagraha,* or true noncooperation, we do not resist or cooperate with it, but ride it and allow it.

19. This will have the effect of enlarging our consciousness, our *prana* (energy) and *prajna* (wisdom).

20. It will redress the balance between our personal self and our impersonal self (since both are needed to be an awakening person) and allow us to stand in this third place, a person-with-and-without-history, a

> When we see all beings in this way, our heart opens. When we see ourselves in this way, we become wise.

temporary magnificence in the face of the faceless absolute.

21. It also sets up the conditions for change, even of the hell-realm itself.

22. The immersion in direct energy of this type takes a flexible and healing ego as its psychological foundation.

23. This is work best done in person over a long period of time. But here is an exercise to contemplate since we cannot meet face-to-face:

Exercise

1. Visualize a devil (first) and an angelic presence (later, on a second try) without emotional intensification or fear but in as great detail as you can manage.

2. You should not picture or visualize a living person with whom you have not yet worked through unfinished feelings. Instead, pick something or someone that scares you. For example: what would happen, moments after you die, if (and here, fill in the blank . . .) appeared? Good. Now picture that devil. You can invent.

3. Now drop all conceptualizations: this being is neither good, nor bad. It is what it is. Do not project any feelings on it.

4. Turn your attention to yourself: how are you different, and in what way?

5. Allow this to continue for a few moments.

6. Now, retract all of your sensory or imaginal contact. Bring your vision back to your own body, your thoughts back to your own brain, your awareness of sound back to your own body . . . and so on.

7. There is nothing here to meditate on. Meditate on it.

8. Simply be with this state of being.

9. Notice that there is a sort of silence that is not quite silent, a hum you cannot easily describe, a subtle light that illuminates more than objects. Different people will have different ways of expressing what is there.

10. Remain with this *light* or *hum* or *silence*.

Dying to the Self

1. As we return from our unconscious human excursion into neuroses (to the extent that we allow the energy of these artifacts to exist without fear and without identifying with them as "our self"), something the 17th-century German mystic Jakob Böhme called "dying to the self" occurs. What does this mean?

2. Let me quote from Böhme.* I've edited his words for the sake of clarity and brevity:

    > *In the hunger the spirit with the body is generated and in the same hunger it goes into its eternal being, unless it breaks its first hunger and brings itself into another.[. . .]*

    > *Death is the only means whereby the spirit may enter into another source and form. If it dies to its selfhood and breaks its will in death, then a new twig springs forth out of the same, but not according to the first will, but according to the eternal will.*

    > *For if a thing enters into its nothing, then it falls again to the creator, who makes that thing as it was known in the eternal will, before it was created to a creature. This is the right aim of eternity, and has no disturbance for it is nature's end.*

    > *Whatever runs on in nature torments itself. But that which attains nature's end, the same is in rest without source and with only one desire.[. . .]*

---

* Jakob Böhme, *Dialogues on the Supersensual Life*, Forgotten Books, 2017.

> *Whatever God is in himself, that the creature is also in its desire in him; a God-angel and God-man, God all in all and without him nothing else. As it was before the times of this world in his eternal harmony, so also it continues in the creaturely voice in him in his eternity and this is the beginning and end of all things.*

3. When we can hold the opposites of our nature, not through egoic strength or denial, but because we have *accepted our true nature with kindness and tenderness,* when we have faced our imperfections and surrendered to the fact that, though they will change to some extent, they are part and parcel of our very being. Our very being, seen in this way, is what makes us divine, is what makes us part of the universe beyond our limited human understanding. Then we drop all "sources" *(i.e., attachments to one pole or the other of opposites)* and center in on one source: our desire for illumination and freedom.

4. This state allows us to relate to each opposite in its natural state as well. This perspective is the realm of the street, the marketplace where the voyager sets up shop.

5. The foundational desire to do this is itself *freedom.*

6. This is the beginning of power, and the voyager needs to work with this every day.

7. In this way the voyage and everything we find there is not constrained by the labels we give views of reality we often call

"personal" or "impersonal," but we use whatever is necessary to continue the healing of self and other.

8. Now we are working in the realm of true nonduality and the power it brings to heal on every level of being. We are unafraid to speak as we are directed because those directions, and the reality that speaks them, form the basis of our own body's and mind's desire, the foundational desire of that area of the All we call the personal self.

9. The nondual voyager—gazing into the unknowable and bringing back gifts—does not make something out of nothing but is content to make something fine from this world, to take the unhealed and expose its holiness, to take the dissonant and find music, to take life as it is and find more life. This is the job and the glory.

Afterword

> *There are intelligent forces that live through us in strange and illogical ways. If you are a shaman, you must leave yourself alone. Stop judging yourself. You don't know what's happening to you and you don't know why it is happening. Furthermore, you must never find out. When something strange happens to you or to a friend or to the world, you want to go and find out why. But in the end, you come back filled with superstition. In searching for answers to the unknowable, human beings ended up in the pool of superstition. In the process of trying to get out of it, they only got deeper into it. From the pool of superstition, they escaped to the desert of skepticism where they died very lonely and miserable deaths without knowing anything about this amazing thing we call life. Let the power ebb through you.*
> —Vusamazulu Credo Mutwa, Zulu Healer

My Mother lives in the unsolvable. In fact, she only exists in the unsolvable. Anyplace else you think she might live, well, that's a myth. Or if not exactly a myth, then what lives there is her shadow. Her shadow can be different than she is, or present things in a different way. Shadow-mother can be warmer than the Mother is, even nicer. Sometimes we prefer this shadow of love to the real thing. But if you are a voyager, you need to meet Mother in her own territory, the only domain she exists in, in the uncontainable way she lives.

This domain where she lives is not a place at all, since all of reality, every bit of it, high and low, good and bad, is shot-through with this un-locatable place, this place that has no address but where we all long to be.

We can never solve the problem of how to get there. It is unsolvable. Only by relating directly to this impossible task can we join with the unsolvable and live this life of spirit. Where is the domain of space if space is everywhere? Where does time live if everything is time?

It is easy to forget the unsolvable. That's because it is inconvenient to meet the unsolvable every day at breakfast. It's a pain in the ass, frankly. We would like, just once maybe, to be left alone. But we cannot be left alone. We were built, you and I, to walk toward the friction of the world, finding sometimes flame and sometimes light, to seek our freedom there. Meeting the unsolvable in the myriad things of each day, we find the place from which the healing of our self and others takes place. Wrestling with the unsolvable makes us intelligent and kind.

Years ago I gave a series of lectures in a small church community center in New Jersey. Since they all took place on Friday nights, we referred to them as the Friday Night Lectures. The first one I gave was called "The Presence of the Unsolvable."

Here are a few excerpts:

> *The beginning of every venture, whether personal or communal, is filled with a passion for solving problems. On the personal path, we solve the problems of our soul, our neurosis, our twists and turns, and we edge toward enlightenment. We become more aware. On the communal path, we learn to live together and have unified goals. Collectively, we learn to work with conflict, allowing many voices to speak in order to afford dignity and respect to all. But the unsolvable problem still lies silently at the center of each of our lives, waiting to speak its mysterious lesson.*
>
> *Even in its mute form, this unsolvable piece makes us uncomfortable. We don't speak about it. We avoid it to the extent that we are actually unaware that it is even there.*
>
> *The ego—which is the problem-solving part of our psyche—does not want to know about the unsolvable. It does not even allow the thought of it to come to the surface of the mind. It is deeply threatening to the ego's sense of its self. The ego's mantra is "If we just work hard enough, are clever enough, spiritual enough, healthy enough, and so on, we will be able to solve whatever problem we come up against."*

AFTERWORD

In its unhealed state, the ego's primary and even sole concern is control. This egoic, can-do approach is central to many of the ways we do the business of life. The entire scientific paradigm is based on this presumption: We don't know now, but we will in the future. And this attitude is coded into the egoic approach to everything we do, including the spiritual search.

[. . . .]

At the core of the spiritual quest, there is a monument to Nothing. This "Nothing" is the state beyond conceptualization, the state that cannot be figured out. However, it is also the state that can be realized. Each person needs to walk the road of spirit and eventually come to this monument and make obeisance. Each person needs to bow down. The inscription on this monument reads, "I stand for Nothing. Feed all of your hopes and dreams into me and they will sink like a stone into silent and dark waters. I hold the key to the world for you." This is the monument to the unsolvable human condition.

True joy is impossible without the confrontation and resolution of your personal conflict with this Nothingness that has no solution and cannot be reduced to "something." If this is not done, a gigantic presence will lurk there, even though it is surrounded by screens and covered with sheets. If we don't personally deal with it, the spiritual path we walk will go around in circles, circling this question the way we would circle a bog or some other impenetrable and unpalatable body of water.

This is true because at the center of all—after all is said and done, after the experiences that give us deep insight and personal power, after the moments of full-throated life—at the center is silence and mystery. It is simply there and there is nothing we can do about it.

The ego dislikes this mystery and vows to conquer it. But the heart— that part of us that can see the world for what it is—loves it. The closer the heart holds mystery to itself, the stronger the heart gets, the bigger it gets until it can contain all of life, that mysterious way-station between silence and more silence. This part of us waits for us when we have grown weary of escape, or have been beaten down by

> *suffering enough so that we come to our senses and embrace the What-Is.*
>
> *[. . . .]*
>
> *We must become one with the unsolvable to the point where we no longer struggle with its truth, but hold it fully and vividly, understanding that it is completely alive and has no solution. Only the unsolvable puts us in touch with the Emptiness or Singularity that cannot be reduced, which contains no thing, and which is beyond illusion. Only the unsolvable lets us look at the core of things, where God is found, and finally, to every periphery where God is as well. Until then, we are struggling in a paper bag, trying to get out of the bottom when the top is open to the sky.*

I've called this "Mother" many other names throughout this book, but here I want to emphasize the flavor of all this, this source that combines clarity and impeccability with the straightforward unending kindness that heals. Warmth and diamond-hard brilliance.

This would be a dualistic concept if there were a person or a place called "the Mother." But there is not. What can you call a place that is everywhere? The Mother, the name of the omnipresent sea the nondual voyager swims in, makes itself known through skillful means in time until it opens into *everywhere* and *everywhen*, its universal accessibility a sign of its unending compassion.

At a certain point, everything springs from the knowledge of who we are. Morality ceases to be an external code; healing stops being something we do instead of something we are; we find we are made of love instead of only searching for bits of lovely feelings to appear in the wreckage of our childhood or our incomplete adulthood. Our empowerment comes from allowing light to be cast on who we are.

Be who you are. Allow it all to come into the light. The light will heal what is broken, yet brokenness—part of the totality of our being—will still remain visible. But now, transformed from shadow and shame, annihilation and despair, they will show themselves as the handmaidens of wholeness, vital participants in the whole affair.

Even the most lowly and base aspects of your personal self can become a means to an end, the end being the healing of yourself and others in the co-arising light of true nonduality, where our imperfections *are* our skills, and our skills, finely honed, are filled with love.

I wish you the very best.

Appendix One: Languages

Opening Your Eyes (and Ears, Nose and Toes) in the Territory and What to Do if You Are Different

1. Because the native territory of all *voyaging* takes place in the realm of the ego,* we are all apt to act too quickly when we voyage to assemble a usable picture that we want to put to immediate use.

2. This is not only because the ego likes useful and practical things and actions—that can be good, of course—but also because this same ego does *not* like uncertainty. In voyaging as I have described it, the ego swims in a sea of uncertainty. That is *its* native home. The unhealed ego does not like to hang out in the unknown—except when it thinks that the "unknown" is a good place to hide from uncertainty! It never works.

3. This is an occupational hazard of being human. But there is help.

---

* This is an interesting point: All of the work of nondual voyaging takes place in the relative world. We might say that in this work we have *turned* to the relative world, secure in the knowledge that it is as whole as some imagined absolute. We see—after long and hard work—that the relative world must always co-arise with the absolute; as voyagers, we no longer lean back to gather words or "moves" that bring up the language of the absolute or even nonduality. Things are just as they are, and we are in the marketplace once and for all. Because of this, the distinctions we might have made in the past about the difference between so-called allopathic and homeopathic approaches are no longer operative. We take upon ourselves the great responsibility of changing things that need changing, fixing those things that need fixing, of even *telling* our clients what they need to do next. Obviously, this is a dramatic sea-change, and I would not trust anyone to do this type of work who did not have specific and distinctive self-knowledge and knew who was speaking in any given moment. This is master-level work.

4. It might be useful at this point to break down the act of voyaging on the inner, visual level by re-framing the map before we enter the territory itself. We will come to see that these examples can be used by people who do not approach voyaging purely through the kinesthetic-visual sense ("seeing-touch") but bring in other sensory modalities.

5. Let's put it another way: If we allow even a little structure around and within this voyaging process—not being afraid of distinctions or disciplines—it is possible to support this excursion into the unknown and unknowable without trying to make it over in some other image. In other words, the addition of these possible structures or "languages" will not limit the voyage to a particular pigeon-hole, but actually broaden and set it free by a process of inspiration, the way breathing in a particular fragrance sets the mind free to ponder, the way Proust's *madeleine* evoked the entire history of his life and times.

6. The *small* evokes the large. The particular, the universal.

7. So, for example, if the legend on a map gives us a sense of distance, we will know how close or far away things are from each other. In essence, the legend not only informs us of something we might already know we want to know but *suggests* to us to look at *distance* as one of the interesting parameters that are possible to consider. We are, in essence, pointed to another level of understanding in the wide-open field of the possible.

APPENDIX ONE: LANGUAGES

8. If this map's legend could depict feelings, tones or thoughts, for example, we would see which feelings, tones or thoughts were close together or farther apart. We would begin to notice if there were clusters of similar feelings or thoughts (or actions or colors and so on) or if the antipodes of feelings or thoughts were what drew them spatially or dimensionally closer to, or further away from, each other in this depiction or, in our case, this voyage.

9. This would bring fresh associations and actually *free* the mind from its own inclinations and prejudices. Here *suggested structures and fresh dimensional thinking* are what free us.

10. Further, if this legend could find the words or symbols to tell us how to move in time or space, in height or depth, we would now know to look for those parameters as well. We would be painting a picture that would have not one or two possible routes of association, detail and density of information, but three or four or five dimensions.

11. Each re-framing would broaden our abilities and slow us down until we can "see the sights" with eyes wide-open and not as an accidental tourist.

12. They would limit the uninformed ego and thus take away its impatience to "get going," or perhaps reduce it substantially. It is an essentially *curious* stance.

13. This process takes voyaging out of the realm of personal preference-*only* and instead

helps us enter—with the help of this self-same ego—a land where self and other meet, a land that was not the imperialist conquest of our unhealed parts making the world over in our own image, but a recognition of the forces that made us who we are—and made the person we are working with as well. The forces that made the world, in other words.

14. I have made a list of some of the dimensional frames or languages we can begin to look for.

15. This list comes from mystical Judaism, Buddhism, architectural theory, visual grammar in the discipline of graphic design, psychotherapeutic theory, biblical thoughts and thoughts about time and space.

16. Once you get the hang of it, you can add your own instruments of investigation, your own list of mental suggestions so that you can see reality assemble itself with as little interference from you as possible—though this assemblage will *always* filter itself through your being, knowledge, heart and spirit—which is as it should be. Now we are using our egos to voyage in the proper way.

APPENDIX ONE: LANGUAGES

Pattern Language

1. The first dimensional frame or language is from architect Christopher Alexander's *A Pattern Language.** Here is an excerpt from the Introduction:

   In this book, we present one possible pattern language, [. . .] This language is extremely practical. [. . .] The elements of this language are entities called patterns. Each pattern describes a problem which occurs over and over again in our environment, and then describes the core of the solution to that problem, in such a way that you can use this solution a million times over, without ever doing it the same way twice.

2. I am presenting some lists of patterns for an entirely different reason, however, namely because of what they do to consciousness—which is tied directly to the language we use and the way we use it—when the list is read to yourself or, perhaps especially, aloud.

3. Because they are *patterns*—and eternally human patterns at that—they do not make sense in the way language usually makes sense. They are not sentences; they do not bring up a particular narrative-building urge; they are not poetry: they cannot be "condensed" into anything other than what they are. In fact, it is their *irreducibility* that is their main feature. They are utterly concrete and yet have emotional and spiritual implications.

---

* Christopher Alexander et al., *A Pattern Language*, Oxford University Press, 1977.

4. We would have to say they are more like *furniture* than words. They sit there like lawn chairs on the grass or an *armoire* in the bedroom, or even a jumbled mixture of tables and chairs in some basement storeroom, piled high in disuse.

5. And yet, in some strange manner, reality seems to understand these patterns and to gather or organize itself around these words.

6. The idea here would be to allow these odd words and phrases to affect you, free your old habit of mind so that you could see the voyaging world freshly.

7. I've listed some of these patterns (which Alexander goes on to describe in architectural terms, something we will not do) in CAPITAL letters, to conform to the way he prints them in his book. There are many more than the ones I've picked out.

- INDEPENDENT REGIONS
- THE DISTRIBUTION OF TOWNS
- CITY COUNTRY FINGERS
- AGRICULTURAL VALLEYS
- COUNTRY TOWNS
- THE COUNTRYSIDE
- ECCENTRIC NUCLEUS
- DENSITY RINGS
- ACTIVITY NODES
- PROMENADE
- SHOPPING STREET
- NIGHT LIFE
- INTERCHANGE
- PATHS AND GOALS
- ACTIVITY POCKETS

APPENDIX ONE: LANGUAGES

- STAIR SEATS
- SOMETHING ROUGHLY IN THE MIDDLE
- INTIMACY GRADIENT
- TAPESTRY OF LIGHT AND DARK
- A PLACE TO WAIT
- SLEEPING TO THE EAST
- COUPLE'S REALM
- RECEPTION WELCOMES YOU
- BUILDING EDGE
- SETTLED WORK
- CONNECTION TO THE EARTH
- THICK WALLS
- HALF-OPEN WALL
- SUNNY COUNTER
- CHILD CAVES
- SECRET PLACE
- SITTING CIRCLE
- MARRIAGE BED
- THE FIRE

8. If you challenge your mind to remain still while reading these evocative words, you will find your consciousness changed and thus your ability to stay in the voyaging state enhanced. Language can deaden or freshen the mind. Breathe these phrases in and let them sit in your body and make new roads and pathways to the infinite.

9. Alexander's book is worth reading, as is his magnum opus, *The Nature of Order*, a work of particular genius.

Visual Grammar

1. The second frame (or language) comes from Christian Leborg's *Visual Grammar*,* which is principally a book of visual concepts for designers. But I found in them a powerful language that shows us the nuances—which many of us who are not committed to being designers—might miss.

2. His visual language is concise, evocative and endlessly interesting. Here, for example, is a little drawing he made on the title page of the book:

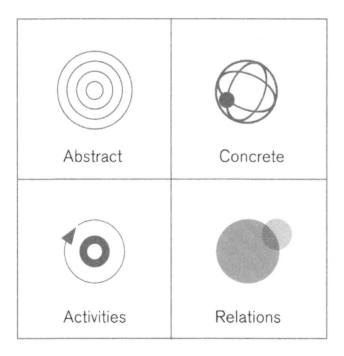

3. If you contemplate these little drawings for a moment, taking each one as a paradigm for voyaging, you have added to your mental vocabulary a number of layered and

---

* Christian Leborg, *Visual Grammar*, Princeton Architectural Press, 2013.

nuanced frames that you can *begin to notice* as you voyage. These frames don't have to be exclusively visual: think for a moment about how they might apply to odor or smell, or touch or thought. You can even bring up *bucolic mind* and see what the "field" looks like as you walk through it thinking of *abstract, concrete, activities* and *relations*. Each one of these words will bring the totality of the field into greater focus while simultaneously expanding the field of perception.

4. Leborg's *Grammar* is especially interesting because it is *visual:* it is not language-based in the ordinary sense. Each of his drawings allows for new relationships—or rather, relationships we were not conscious of—to appear in our bodymindspirit.

5. Here for example is his opening page for the drawing labeled *abstract:*

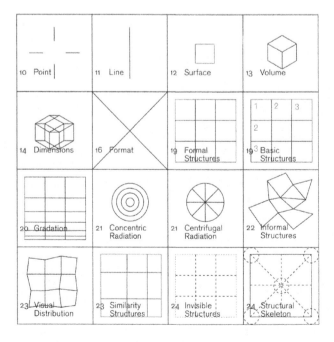

6. Here is one possible way to use this visual chart: What would it be like if, when voyaging, you remembered some of these terms? For example: *surface*. Surfaces can be dull, shiny, textured, smooth, bumpy, metallic, organic, matrixed and embossed; they can be concave, convex, have depressions or have extrusions. If you were gazing at water or crystal or had learned to gaze at air and have the same entry into voyaging, these words would come in handy.

7. To use another of Leborg's images, *volume:* things (images, smells, tastes . . . even thoughts and feelings) can have little or no volume (less or more intensity?), be three-dimensional or imply other, hidden volumes and therefore other dimensions, complex or simple.

8. So too with centrifugal radiation and concentric radiation and informal structures, gradation, invisible structures and so on.

9. Just a little while ago, I took a break from writing these notes and went to do some errands. It is raining today and unseasonably warm. While it should be around 30°F, it is approaching 68°F. Yet the trees are bare, and the colors are the colors after Fall: the reds and browns have given way to wet blacks, grey skies and surprisingly green grass. As I walked through the light rain, I thought about *surface,* and *invisible structures.* I wondered if the rain fell equally on all things, my head, the trees, and so on. Normally, I would just answer that question logically: of course it falls equally on all things! Yet, entering this *turn,* I wondered if

there was another, perhaps invisible structure that organized the distribution of rain in some other way. Then I thought about *graduation:* was the rain of the same density in all places? Or was there something irregular about the way *densities* of rain arranged themselves? Could I hear the rhythm of these densities, softer then louder, then softer, then a whisper? What was the music?

10. Doing all this didn't help me actually answer these questions, but it opened my sight—my inner sight—to the fact that this day seemed to be about openings into new vistas, new doorways to pass through, new places—inner and outer—to explore.

11. When the ground is prepared correctly, the plant breaks the surface of the ground as suddenly as a laugh. Without understanding this background, you would not understand the hard work that goes on underground before the budding shoot breaks the surface of the earth.

12. My senses became mixed: I touched the visual; I thought sound. Time and space changed too: I explored the future from the vantage point of the present.

13. The sense was that this opening into something new was valid for me and many others. It was not just a generalization (i.e., things are always opening up into something new if you pay attention, after all) but, from the perspective of *continuity/density,* I had travelled "someplace" and brought back this message of positive exploration. If I had had healing

clients on this day, I'm sure it would have come up.

14. Of course, none of this is earthshaking. No great revelations about the cosmic strings of the universal heart, but rather, something small was uncovered. A path through the woods on a rainy day. Sometimes that's enough.

15. Because Leborg is a master of visual relationship (which is, after all, what a *grammar* does: relate one thing to another . . .) his work is rich and filled with possibility.

16. The main thing to understand is that we are dealing here with information, but information seen anew because we are *changing states*.

17. What I mean by this is that whenever data from one discipline or media is transferred to another, the information is not simply duplicated but *changed* by the transition itself.

18. Although people might like to believe that there is some objective process whereby things can enter new form and retain the same parameters, exude the same thoughts and ideas, this is not so.

19. When we change "shapes," we learn something new. An example: if you displayed the connections between individual internet users and the sites they visited as a list of numbers and letters, you would see a certain relationship emerge. It might be hierarchical, such as *here are the top*

ten sites visited by people. But if the same information were formed as a visual graph with dots and lines, what would emerge would be the organic spider-web of connections that are within the information.

20. So what would have changed would have been *which layers of the collage became vivid and which receded.* We would see what was important and what was not. New relationships come into focus, and new levels of meaning begin to surface.

21. Because of this, you might see, for example, that this same organic spider-web also relates to voter patterns and transportation hubs and language and DNA and so on. George Zipf did this in his remarkable book, *Human Behavior and the Principle of Least Effort,*[*] when he charted the appearance of certain words in all languages. Because his work was, let us say, in the morph of the world, scientists many years later began to see a *linguistic pattern* in parts of DNA, thought at that time to be aimless and patternless.

22. For our purposes, by allowing our journeying to be re-imagined in other forms *as we do it,* we are inviting in a multitude of levels, inviting the scene to be perceived or smelled or sensed in some other way, to be enriched and thereby to become *denser within the continuity.*

---

[*] George Zipf, *Human Behavior and the Principle of Least Effort,* Martino Fine Books, 2012.

23. We then get to "tune" to different vividnesses, ones we might have missed without these new maps.

24. Finally, I'd like to add a list of some words that Leborg uses as part of a basic vocabulary for images aimed at graphic designers. We, on the other hand, are going to use them for what they evoke as we look into the mystery within which our voyage takes place. I've added some words of my own, and I have not distinguished between Mr. Leborg's words and my own. They are not meant to stand opposite each other or to make pairs. They are simply "locations" to be considered as you walk through voyaging's pathless light:

    - starting point
    - ending point
    - structure line
    - structure unit
    - tactile
    - tangent
    - displaced
    - convergent
    - diffusion
    - exact, precise
    - tone
    - texture

25. My associations with these words are often not the associations Mr. Leborg gives. For me, they are suggestions whispered in the night; whether I roll over and touch them depends upon my dreams.

26. I am indebted to Christian Leborg for his brilliant insights and beautiful book.

Skandhas

1. All of these "languages" are really perspectives on, or new ways to organize the present and to think about information. In our case, we are thinking about how to alleviate human suffering.

2. Each additional level of organization allows new associations, brings new insights and broadens our contact with reality-as-it-is.

3. Much of Buddhism's re-visioning of the human condition of suffering has to do with seeing through ordinary consciousness' sense of the ego as a separate and continuous entity so that an underlying reality, which is free of ownership and the continuous sense of an "I," can present itself to our awareness.

4. The *skandhas*—the Sanskrit word for *aggregate* or *bundle* or *heap*, and consisting of *material form, feelings, perception, volition* and *sensory awareness*—are, according to Buddhist thinking, the assemblages that constitute what a human being is. This is the scaffolding on which we build our sense of a personal self.

5. The Theravada tradition sees clinging to these aggregates or heaps as the cause of suffering. The Mahayana tradition, going further, asks us to understand that the *skandhas* do not independently arise but are connected to the co-arising sense of an "I." In all cases, however, it is the clinging to these aggregates that causes all suffering. To quote from the Pali canon:

> ...*The noble disciple . . . does not regard form [or other aggregates] as self, or self as possessing form, or form as in self, or self as in form. That form of his changes and alters. Despite the change and alteration of form, his consciousness does not become preoccupied with the change of form. . . . Through non-clinging he does not become agitated.*
> [Wikipedia]

6. From a Buddhist point of view, these *skandhas* are problematic in that they form an almost solid and believable structure, which creates a sense of being that feels it is only an ego. This ego does not understand that it is created simply by the interaction of the environment and these *heaps* or assemblages. This identification with an "I" is what causes most of our suffering.

7. Let me quote liberally from the Rigpa Wiki* (an online encyclopedia of Tibetan Buddhism):

   > *Sogyal Rinpoche wrote: Once we have a physical body, we also have what are known as the five skandhas—the aggregates that compose our whole mental and physical existence. They are the constituents of our experience, the support for the grasping of ego, and also the basis for the suffering of samsara.*

   And Chögyam Trungpa Rinpoche said†:

   > *The five skandhas represent the constant structure of the human psychology as well as*

---

* *www.rigpawiki.org*
† *The Collected Works of Chögyam Trungpa, Vol.2*, Shambhala Publications, 2010.

> *its pattern of evolution and the pattern of the evolution of the world. The skandhas are also related to blockages of different types—spiritual ones, material ones, and emotional ones.*

8. Since part of Buddhism is the practice of examining what the self actually is, these *skandhas* are a discovery of sorts for the origin of this ghostly part of our consciousness—indeed our consciousness itself in many ways—that we call a personal self.

9. The full understanding of the *skandhas* is quite complex, as it involves not only the actual sense organs themselves and the information they impart to consciousness, but also involves how they help form consciousness itself as the "current" this sensory information rides on, and even how this current and the objects of consciousness interact.

10. The *skandhas* also represent the attraction we have toward types of feelings, sensations and states of consciousness, and the aversion we have toward these same things.

11. By investigating the sense of self through meditation, the spiritual seeker can actually slow down automatic mental processes, see them in action, so to speak, and thereby soften or break the belief in a continuous sense of self that actually depends upon these *skandhas*, which come and go and are not continuous at all. This gives us perspective as to what the "I" sense actually is.

12. Depending upon which level of *skandhas* we are talking about, the lists of words associated with them are quite extensive. For example:

    The Five Skandhas:

    Feeling
    Perception
    Formations
    Consciousness
    Form

    The Six Consciousnesses:

    Visual (or eye) consciousness
    Auditory (or ear) consciousness
    Olfactory (or nose) consciousness
    Gustatory (or tongue) consciousness
    Tactile (or body) consciousness
    Mental (or mind) consciousness

    The Six Sense Objects
    (or Six Outer Sources):

    sights
    sounds
    smells
    tastes
    textures
    mental objects

    The Six Sense Faculties
    (or Six Inner Sources):

    eyes
    ears
    nose
    tongue
    body
    mind

APPENDIX ONE: LANGUAGES

13. The major point I would like to make about all of these words, however, is that for our purposes, the *skandhas* are only a problem *at first. This understanding is quite important for the nondual voyager.*

    The difference between the Buddhist view and the perspective from nondual voyaging

14. When the student has made progress in separating from the automatic belief in a self—a sense of self as a "who I am," as something unchanging and solid—these same *skandhas* reveal a deeper level.

15. The *skandhas* are then *not* seen as problematic, but rather as a *resource* for further exploration into *bucolic mind*, through the understanding of *continuity/density*.

16. From the point of view of true nonduality, which does not split the world in any way, we understand that this *self-sense* we call our ego-personality is one part among all the parts of the natural world. We see that it is a valid, important part of our lives, especially as it heals and reveals more and more of its true nature: as part of creation. The need to "see through it," destroy it, see it only as an illusion, disappears. It is, after all, an important partner in our spiritual search and not only the impediment it is sometimes characterized as being.

    Living in a world of allies

17. Through the awareness of *continuity/density*, we can allow our consciousness of the *skandhas* to coexist with the sense of a personal self as mutually-arising creations, each valid and each dependent upon the other.

18. Because of this insight, we can now *selflessly inhabit the sensual world that we call home* while being a personal being, especially with the further understanding that even the sense of a personal self is something created by the universe itself. It is not a perversion of our destiny, and, when healed, is the perfect vehicle—indeed the only vehicle— to take us to what wholeness actually means.

19. Healing this ego rather than trying to transcend, ignore or destroy it, brings us to a place in which all of who we are is important.

20. The sensual world—this world of red dust— then becomes a place of wonder, information, gathering, dispersing, moving and standing still. In short, the rightful home of the person who is now a "personal person created by the great impersonal forces."

21. As my wife and teacher likes to say, Oneness is not the only miracle: the fact that we are separate, that we see ourselves as beings who have identity, is a miracle as well. Oneness and separateness, both illuminated.

22. Nondual voyaging is a discipline based on being here, right where we are. There is no place else to escape to.

23. Nondual voyaging is an effort based solely and directly on this world. Even though it makes excursions into *subtle dimensions,* these dimensions are firmly in the world of duality. Though we are aware of their underpinnings in the absolute, we relate

directly to the black, whites and grays of this world.

24. Most paradoxically, if we relate to the *skandhas* in this way—at one moment understanding the eye that sees, the next moment the sight-object it sees, watching as a sense of self arises from sensations and perceptions—and if we are sensitive enough to feel each separately and then the consciousness that arises when they co-arise, *we become whole people, seated in a true, impersonal unity that includes the personal self, working with the world as it is.*

> The *skandhas* are the syntax makers. The object is not to pretend we can get free of all contexts, but to awaken to them and reclaim our ability to choose.

25. We no longer need to think about "the whole," "the larger picture," or the difference between allopathic or homeopathic perspectives. The world becomes a playground and "shamanic playfulness" something we can master with continual effort.

26. Then we no longer need to worry about "aversion" or "attachment." Both aversion and attachment become different pieces of furniture in a room of the world, each interesting in itself, each "on the table" of being. We begin to understand the miracle of these conglomerates, these heaps and bundles, and their almost magical ability to create a space called "self" and the unlimited contents of that unlimited space.

27. This self is as holy as any other thing in the world, and with it we can touch an intimate, sensuous life filled with tones, colors, cooling waters and the song of birds.

Learning, Finding and Inventing Other Languages

1. The main idea I am trying to share here is how we might use frames from one discipline or perspective by transferring them to or overlaying them on the frame we are using or inhabiting.

2. This is a form of synesthesia—the "production of a sense impression relating to one sense or part of the body by stimulation of another sense or part of the body"—only as a *chosen* methodology or path instead of something bestowed by some personal biology.

3. These various frames help us remember to broaden our perspective. They create a kind of X-ray vision that can see through one layer of reality for the purpose of allowing another to come forth, organizing reality in yet a different way. Here is another that occurred to me: The Torah talks about the "four rivers of Eden." Here is the verse in Genesis:

   > *A river flowed out of Eden to water the garden, and there it divided and became four rivers. The name of the first is Pishon; it is the one which flows around the whole land of Havilah, where there is gold; and the gold of that land is good; bdellium and onyx stone are there. The name of the second river is Gihon; it is the one which flows around the whole land of Cush. And the name of the third river is Tigris, which flows east of Assyria. And the fourth river is the Euphrates.*

4. This verse has interested seekers over the years for purely materialistic reasons: they wanted to pinpoint the physical location of Eden.

5. My approach—and my need—were somewhat different. Looking at the meanings of the names of these rivers, I found additional metaphors, if you will, with which to overlay my consciousness while in the *turn*, walking through the field of reality.

6. In this case, Pishon means "increase/meandering," while Gihon means "bursting or gushing forth." Tigris means "rapid," while Euphrates means "fruitful."

7. Pishon helped me remember to meander. It was very easy for me to try to get to the end before I was at the beginning. Meandering is the truth of this path and not something extra.

8. When I remembered to meander, things began to "gush forth": ideas, associations, connections. In essence, I found myself in the River Tigris with its rapid movement and then in the Euphrates' bountifulness.

9. I understood these rivers not as myth but as map. A map about a process of returning to Eden while still in the land of Nod. Nod means "to wander," and, while in Torah exegesis it is thought of as a form of exile, I chose to think of it as the pattern of human life as we move through time and space and live out our allotted years.

10. The point is to set up associative thinking, not so much for "getting under" something in a psychological way but for seeing the network of reality, Indra's Web, as the underlying information gradient or structure behind the separate manifestations.

11. When I played back and forth between these underlying roots and "how things were" in the field of being . . . answers came.

12. Other languages might include the following parameters:

    - the languages of *time* and *space*
    - the languages of *different speeds* and *kinds of movement*
    - the language of dance—ballet, for example—with its clearly delineated positions and movements
    - the language of ecology, which can have interactive, deeply nested and matrix-like inter-relational imagery.
    - the language of chaos theory and fractals
    - the language of feelings and emotions

13. These languages are all in my knapsack as I walk out into the field, enjoying a rainy day as much as a clear one, being clear myself or foggy, happy or sad, but always ready to receive the goodness of the earth.

Appendix Two: The Astral Realm and What is Real

1. I'd like to say a few brief words about the realms in which nondual voyaging takes place. I'm mentioning this now simply because I'd like to give each voyager a few inner tools with which to monitor themselves as they journey, with an eye toward keeping the material that emerges from this nondual approach authentic and truly helpful.

2. My intention in not bringing some of this up before was to protect the student's clean slate, that is, to not announce where we were "going" but rather give instructions for *states of consciousness,* which the student could use to arrive in the space where the work takes place. My concern in naming these states too early was that this might run the risk of predisposing the student toward one idea or another as to what these realms would reveal or what they might be like. This would limit the large field in which I wanted the nondual voyager to play.

3. The astral realm—which many students of spirituality are familiar with—is an example of such a limiting concept.

4. The astral plane, as it is commonly thought of, a metaphysical location that is often seen as the realm in which shamanism takes place, is a kind of "not here." In other words, it is seen as another realm, separate from our physical life, a subtle and metaphysical place where shadow versions

of our lives take place. It is also intensely tied up with the concept of forces that are also "not here," but that can affect our lives for good or ill. We then, from this point of view, are at the mercy of this astral plane and need specialists who can interact with this plane to help us.

5. For many healers and shamans, then, everything that follows and takes the form of healing has the potential to be built on this foundation, a foundation that is, from my point of view, problematic.

6. The healing of these potentially negative forces—forces that act on us without our permission—consists mainly of protection of one sort or another. It has the problematic aspect, however, of further institutionalizing the *personal* self and mostly never goes beyond—or into—the origins of this seemingly personal place to see how it is born into our reality.

7. (This emphasis on the personal is immediately a problem since our reality cannot be said to be entirely personal or impersonal, but a co-dependent arising of these two facets.)

8. So the astral plane becomes the place of our hopes (many teachers have likened it to a sort of heaven, filled with freedom from cares) and also our fears and dangers.

9. Once the nondual voyager has dealt with these questions and comes to new understandings that I will expand upon further below, the deeper usefulness of this

APPENDIX TWO: THE ASTRAL REALM AND WHAT IS REAL

place that is actually here, in this single world, becomes apparent.

10. As healers—and as humans—we are all a mixed bag. Because there is a fundamental imbalance in the foundations of this universe (for example, there is more matter in the universe than anti-matter, so that the universe does not seem to be neutral but charged in the direction of *something* rather than *nothing*), everything built on these imbalances follows suit.

11. And though imbalances can be painful in any realm, from psychological to physical, they are always dynamic and interactive. When things are completely equal, we have no interactions but instead a static, undynamic condition.

12. As I mentioned, however, this inequality also leads to problems. All things are imperfect and, in human life, often troublesome: the earth can be unsteady and fate unkind.

13. So anyone who attempts to voyage to find helpful answers to human difficulties will automatically find themselves traversing a field of problems, extensions of their own misconceptions, limitations, wrong conclusions and so on, all built into the system of existence.

14. Only hard work can wake us up to them and, in this way, minimize our being caught by our own misconceptions.

15. Our job as nondual voyagers is to become—in the words of the *Flower Ornament Sutra*—

greatly enlightened as to our delusions. This is what awakening is.

16. Despite every effort we make to escape this potential trap, however, we are all likely to fall into it at one time or another. This inevitability can also be an opportunity to heal and pass our healing on to others.

17. All of the realms the nondual voyager travels in reside in our brains. This might not be fashionable to say these days, especially when people like to talk about "mind" and "spirit" as if they were separate from the physical world.

18. But the nondual voyager is not enticed by such a split: there is no more spiritual realm than right here, in this cage of light.

19. We need to understand that all of these realms exist *functionally* in the brain. The brain is that part of the universe that pulls out of the infinitely subtle myriads of threads and pulsations, those "wavelengths" or "mind-lengths" to which we give all of these lofty names.

20. Seen in this way, "consciousness" is a *location* in physical reality rather than something separate from so-called "objective" reality. It is the location point where a certain type of voyaging takes place and where explorers can gather to see the sights.

21. Having these realms located in the physical brain does not mean that this brain is not imaging something that resides *in every other place in the universe as well*. It simply means:

this is where we see it, in the same way a radio is the place where we participate in sharing thoughts, involving ourselves in a narrative, being entertained or catching up on events in places near and far.

22. Our brain has been formed by evolution, genetics and our early environment. All of these forces actually physically change the myriad of structures and connections in the physical machinery.

23. Changing these structures changes what it can do and how it does it. So what we call "reality" is the sum total of the person who views it through these physical assemblages—a "person" who has been created by these very assemblages themselves.

24. What we take as "reality" is composed of all of these formative structures, superimposed upon whatever we believe is "there." In fact, the very concept of "there," as opposed to "here," is part and parcel of the language the brain has created in order to subsume the full—and impossible to apprehend—spectrum of the plenum. We have even invented—or are the invention of!—a psychic location called "the ego" to demarcate and contrast different locations in our effort to subdue this vastness that might otherwise overwhelm us.

25. We are in a constant state of relational creativity—but artists only when we are awakening to the play of all this in what we call our consciousness.

26. So the cables of our nerves continue to reverberate with evolutionary imperatives, knots and bends created by genetics and neurosis, sustained by early environmental parental factors, and the misguided belief that holding onto these visions is the best way to survive.

27. So awareness is never "pure." It is always expressed as the sum total of the brain's journey and the impact of all of these formative forces.

28. Please note: as we stop using our personal dictionary as the only way to decipher the world around us, all of this becomes our raw material, our *prima materia,* our unending resource with which to form the perceptions of healing. All we need at first is to awaken to these truths.

29. These resources include, of course (and maybe even especially), our neurotic patterns, since imperfection is ubiquitous. When we are unaware of our imperfections, others suffer. Aware of them, we suffer but also have—as we become conscious of them—our concurrent, innate and earthy ability to heal into deeper intimacy with the world.

30. These neuroses become little centers of gravity around which the unhealed or unintegrated ego constructs an image of reality based solely on one of its primary needs: to survive. This mostly unconscious coloration escapes our notice, and it becomes difficult for us to believe that there is any "strategy of living" going on or that

reality has been editorialized rather than reported.

31. The nondual healer is dedicated to understanding all of this and to putting into practice the revealing and healing of these submerged beliefs. Only in this way can healers offer help to others without furthering the injury of those they work with by unconsciously colluding with their client's unhealed ego's view of the world.

32. We live in an infinity of worlds, all of which reside *here*, in this moment, perceivable by this wondrous brain, the universe's Grand Central Station for observing itself.

33. Since this same brain is, as I have said, the sum total of its journey through life—including the injuries, emotional and otherwise, it suffered at the hand of existence—by necessity our vision of what is, and is not, is skewed.

34. The realm in which all of our un-worked-through material is located is the astral plane.

35. When we see this marvelous brain not as the holder of "subjective" material but as the "radio" that picks up material and forms it into a "program," we can begin to understand that *everything that is or can be perceived by this brain or thought of by this brain or imagined by this brain,* when properly understood, is not a personal-*only* event or thing, but the specifics of the totality, the *densities* that co-arise with a vast *continuity*.

36. Certain specifics, such as the war between the ego's desire to survive by controlling its environment and its equal passion to explain, explore and evolve, create a lineage of discontinuity, of imbalance and conflict—problems that, as anything else in the universe, have their own place to reside, to cluster and thereby create their own field in which to gather.

37. The so-called astral plane, a dimension of consciousness that some believe (mistakenly, in my view) figures in many traditional descriptions of shamanism, is such a place. It is a potentially obscuring lens, which can masquerade as a psychic location from which helpful advice—or danger—can emerge. We only believe this is so when we do not fully understand the origin of this dimension of existence and what resides there.

38. We could say that the astral plane is the spiritual dimension populated by the part-objects of the personal. These part-objects are, by definition, not wholes or accurate pictures of the world. Instead they represent a developmental stage that is incomplete in its comprehension of reality, but unaware that it is incomplete. It has no reference point, therefore, to see that it is a partial view.

39. This is why in many spiritual traditions, the astral is often talked about as the home of desires, unfulfilled wishes and nonmaterial beings, running the gamut from angelic presences to demonic ones.

IYI:
Part of a traditional shaman's training is to transform themselves so that what starts out as their own part-objects projected into a so-called "astral realm" reveal themselves to be the spiritual objects they actually are. It is only through this self-transformation that these spiritual objects can be of use.

40. What I want us to keep in mind is that this realm is not whole, holographically or imagistically, and that it is the natural home of *glamour and power*—the other potential pitfalls for the voyager when its origins are not fully understood.

41. This habitat, composed of the unhealed ego's needs, is the miasmatic atmosphere of the developmental problems the voyager—and all of us—have.

42. The unhealed ego—because it unconsciously senses its incompleteness—wants to be seen as a magical being, as someone special, as important and unique in order to avoid its suffering. To do this it *substitutes imagistic wholeness for the real self left behind, unnoticed in the psychic disarray of the poisoned ground*. In this way parts become wholes and echoes become entire stories.

43. The astral plane is therefore also the place where our unhealed narcissism is given free—but mostly unconscious—rein.

44. For most of us, our healthy narcissism as a child was not met with healthy parenting, and so what remains are aspects of our self that live and function in an "as-if" world.

45. When we *voyage*, we are taking a journey. What we perceive, and how we communicate it, can come from wholeness, or, just as easily, from the wounded self.

46. However, in a very real sense, it will always come from *both* the wounded and healing self. The problem arises *when we do not know the difference or confuse one with the other.*

47. The voyager or shaman who is not aware of these pitfalls and problems that make up part of their existence can be said to be living in the astral plane themselves, since after all, the home of the unconscious, unhealed ego *is* the astral plane, where the part-objects of their own consciousness fly around in an unnoticed mist. It is not a realm devoted to introspection but rather to *display*.

48. Communicating from the astral realm, rather than from the perspective of *continuity/density*, has a different flavor and different consequences.

49. These flavors and consequences—because they emanate from unfinished business within the healer, business that the healer is *not aware of* and therefore unconsciously continues to "act out" in their communication—have a different impact on the client. Even if the nondual healer has the same or other imperfections, their communication-from-awareness has a different flavor and different consequences.

50. Here are some of the differences I've found in these two types of communication, nondual and astral:

Astral Communication Is Comparative

51. *Comment:* There is no "thing in itself." Rather, there is always a hidden opposite. For example, protection is needed because the person is in danger as opposed to the nondual view: because the person needs protection, not "from something 'objective' that is trying to do them harm," but because

protection itself, as itself, is needed. It is part of the totality of being.

Astral Communication Begets Inequality

52. *Comment:* When the healer is not aware of their own astral involvement, they cannot see the client—or themselves—clearly, and what may sneak in is the healer's "higher position" as the "one who knows." Even if statements and suggestions are made with humility, there is a flavor that could create additional separation between the healer and client. The nondual view might make the same pronouncements, but the separation factor—because the healer is constantly relating to both souls without the diversion of the astral—is minimized.

Astral Communication Is a Display of Power

53. *Comment:* We only need to display power when we are afraid. When we are unaware of our fear, our display seems real, that is, as if we have real power. The nondual view is that power is owned and accepted but it does not raise the person up; rather, it in a sense lowers them by creating spaciousness and humility and, above all, connectedness. So the nondual voyager can—and must—accept their own relationship with power, but this power does not make anyone else powerless or subordinate.

Astral Communication Is . . . Slightly "Out of Time and Rhythm"

54. *Comment:* The nondual voyager stands in one-hundred percent separation from the client and the client in one-hundred

percent separation from them. Rather than being contradictory to my statement above, this one-hundred percent separation is actually individuation in its most complete sense. Because of this, the nondual voyager does not need the client to complete himself or herself. There is no "fifty-fifty" bargain wherein the unstated deal is "I will complete you as you complete me."

55. When we are truly individuated (not as a defense), we are not avoiding our own suffering and consequently there is no vampire-ish need of someone else's energy to complete our own wholeness. Because of this, it is possible to sense when someone is speaking from the astral—the home of their own unconscious parts—by perceiving that it is slightly "out of step." Finally, when we are "in step," the truth of a mutual, co-arising universe is experienced as a fact. Now, more clear-eyed, we can see when our client is caught by astral images and beliefs, and we can be of aid, since our own fears and unworked-through material are not in the way.

Astral Communication Is Heroic

56. *Comment:* Astral communication is heroic and romanticized. Effort is made in the service of some imagined purity, hard to achieve, difficult to find, which results in things marvelous and amazing. The push is not toward the ordinary—which would uncover the client's own, personal magic—but toward the miraculous and special. This push is, of course, a need of the healer's, which has little to do with the client, unless—when the healer's insight is

> Synchronicity is the nonlinear, holographic world showing its face in ordinary reality.

evolved—the true synchronicities can be seen.

57. By working carefully and faithfully with the concept of *continuity/density,* many of these pitfalls can be avoided, simply because having to take into account simultaneously the continuous, completely connected totality of things *and* the complete separateness and individuation of things, helps relax the ego from the position of the powerful central watcher to one of the components of reality, one that—like all the other realms—is experienced and imaged in the brain. This has the benefit of disentangling the healer from their unhealed ego and clarifying who is speaking—and from where in the psyche speech arises at any given moment.

58. All helpers *must* go through the gates of this problem in order to grow into masters of their discipline. Without the resolution of this problem, narcissistic needs and other remnants of our imperfect upbringing will almost always spill into the relationship between the voyager and the one seeking help.

59. For the voyager who attempts to work in this nondual way, synchronicities appear, inspiration is allowed to sing its song, healing opportunities appear at every corner.

60. The nondual voyager who is practicing this is filled with luck. Happenstance becomes as powerful as logic, the holographic and fractal as important as the linear.

61. The nondual voyager then continues to learn about the inner landscape so that his or her ego (which is, remember, a *density* itself) becomes malleable enough to survive the encounter with the absolute or *continuity*.

62. Then, continuing to heal, their ego becomes healthy enough to hold their *dual nature* as wave *and* ocean, yellow *and* gold, the *particular one* who can never be separated from the undifferentiated part of reality. They live as a *density* in the midst of an infinity of other densities, always in contact with the *continuity*. As we grow in awareness, we grow into the recognition of this state of being.

63. Knowing this truth is awakening to wholeness.

64. Through work on ourselves, we are honest healers.

65. Through communication that holds wholeness, we bring ourselves and our clients to life. We don't create further obstacles to put in their path.

66. We then operate not from the astral but from wholeness.

67. We begin to realize that though we are never free from our distortions, our very awareness of this makes us free. We live in a world where logic is not a constraining feature but an element in the whole, where the linear and the circular and the sporadic live in harmony, in a single ecology.

68. When we do this, we touch the face of truth, we raise Buddha from his sleep, we knock on Heaven's door, we see the world as a glinting jewel.

69. The nondual voyager *is* commitment-in-action and, being that, we can bring forth splendors.

Appendix Three: Reality's Two Sides

1. For the nondual voyager, the world is an analog wave, a *continuity* with peaks and troughs. The peaks and troughs of this wave are the *densities* that appear to us as the world of emptiness and fullness. These peaks and valleys make up the *continuity/density*.

2. As this understanding becomes accessible in the voyager's body, the voyager ceases thinking in terms of archetypes or mythological space.

3. Archetypes and mythological consciousness are the products of a self seen as separate from—but yearning for—wholeness. They are the beautiful circles and lines of a heaven that is still slightly out of reach. This is a subtle consideration.

4. In this example, consciousness has not yet achieved the recognition of the prior wholeness that includes the world *and* the self. Instead, in a heroic and sometimes desperate manner, this consciousness stretches outward (or inward) for a hoped-for unity. It is an explorer in the desert of the separate self, seeking the oasis of the waters of reality.

5. The nondual voyager no longer uses the language of archetypes, and this is one of the crucial differences between the voyager and someone who is not practicing shamanism from a nondual position. (Of course, many traditional shamans—though

they might not use this language—practice and live from a nondual perspective.)

6. For the nondual voyager, it is not so much that mythological space does not exist, but it is "on the table," along with everything else, and not something viewed as a psychological or spiritual place with its own existence, from which the shaman can gather information from a protected position, a position in which the shaman's ego is untutored, untouched, and without co-creative responsibility.

> A good example of this is the way Carlos Castaneda speaks about Don Juan's concept of *seeing*. Carlos discovers that as long as he stands apart from the world, this *seeing*, which is something more than sight, cannot be accomplished. A "man of knowledge" can perceive the world because he or she has perceived themselves. It is not a matter of technique but of attainment.

7. So from this perspective, there is no "lower world," "middle world," or "upper world" as *separate* places. Rather, they are *intensities* or *densities* and not "places."

8. Power animals are no longer the bearers of messages from one *sequestered* self to another—*as if they existed in realms entirely separate from our own and as entirely separate beings as well.*

> Since the voyager is no longer solely operating in the subject/object paradigm, these power animals are neither subjective nor objective. Please consider this.

9. Instead, all of these metaphors exist simultaneously in the same space, brought to the fore only by the voyager's ability to interact with the *density* of each, making vivid one dimension or another for the sake of the one they are voyaging for. Everything is part of a single set. Nothing can stand outside of that set.

10. (This does not mean that these power animals and such are simply projected subjective elements of the voyager's own psyche. This explanation would be one still caught in the subject/object metaphor as something "real," the way things actually

are. The nondual voyager on the other hand, knows that everything is a context, a syntax, and is free to choose the ones that are most skillful and useful. Again, this does not mean that "everything is relative," or that "everything is allowed": the voyager knows how to ride the current of a truth that is not limited by personal preference…and yet includes this element in the totality of reality.)

11. The experienced voyager has dispensed with this nomenclature entirely and sees everything, every realm, as part of the same landscape, including messages and messengers.

12. This final step has the effect of stopping the imposition of the chains of limited psychological thinking upon the plenum of reality, realizing that psychological thinking is a particular filter that adds its own coloration and organization to anything we perceive.

13. We can never be free of ourselves and our sensory and mental abilities. We are just as we are, built of our activities—all of them—as part of a single realm. We are *densities,* the expression of the *continuity* in matter . . . and the *continuity*, the expressive mother of her material and non-material children.

14. The nondual voyager is comfortable in this world of "two sides," this Janus-faced reality where two sides are part of the single being of reality.

15. The voyager is also comfortable with relating to each facet of this reality and

seeing each piece not as a part-object but as an exemplar of the whole.

16. As such, I am describing a practice (nondual voyaging) that takes place within the awakening individual and not as part of the continuing quest that is the preoccupation of the unhealed ego, the one who is still looking for special communication from other entirely separate beings in order to inform his or her separate imagination and to save or authenticate his or her seemingly entirely separate life. The voyager has relinquished that job.

17. In nondual voyaging, even the imagination is a *density* dancing within the *continuity* for its own sake.

18. Though we will forever rise and fall within duality, fail and succeed, forget and remember, for the nondual voyager, this sine wave is the best expression of true wholeness and is embraced in this spirit.

19. There is room for doubt and boredom, for being amazed and enthralled, for entering trance and leaving trance, for being lost as one of the most interesting things in the nature of the self. After all, when we are "lost," where do we really go? *We are lost in the present moment, in* this *time and space.*

20. The passion and color of the heroic journey—here I am thinking of the magnificent mandalas that Carl Jung painted as part of his journey toward wholeness described in the Red Book—is both eliminated by the voyager's sense of

wholeness and replaced by the constantly fertile roiling of the physical world; by "physical world" I even include the mental, inner world, for, after all, its basis is purely physical as well.

21. The voyager looks at this inner world with the same awe with which he or she looks at the snow on the branches of the hickory or the new light green grass sprouting everywhere in spring or the dying raccoon that stumbled up to my deck the other day.

22. This inner world, then, is both totally physicalized and simultaneously united with all other realms. So, instead of archetypes, which still keep a separation between seer and seen, we have the *yantra** of the world that *includes our self*. The storm of reality passes through us constantly in a creative flux, in which life and that part of life called death constantly dance.

---

* The *yantra*, a meditational aid in Hindu Tantra, can be considered a pictorial example of the self, the world, and the cosmos.

23. Where does music start? When I play my flute, does it start with the air inside my body, or with the thought to play the flute itself and the idea of what I might want to play? How about the designers of the instrument itself, who built upon a lineage of thought and materials to make the instrument I have in my hands? And the teachers who taught me and the listener, whether that listener is my own ears or the people who listen and accept this sound into their own bodies?

24. For the voyager—at least some of the time!—all of this is kept in mind and none of it is kept in mind: it is a non-issue, not the point. Now the player can be the music—which we always were anyway, but with no one there especially to care. Again: we do what we do.

25. Nonduality relishes the dual, exults in the separate. The passing of time and the fading away of all things *is* the *continuity-in-action*, a most marvelous, terrible and awe-inspiring thing.

26. The voyager begins to make the leap that will take them out of their own existence and past their own death. The *continuity* is so big, so creative, so abundant in its resources and activity, that new *densities* will constantly be created. The voyager relies on this cornucopia to spill out this ongoing universal, moment by moment.

27. Conversely, the plethora of *densities* allows the *continuity* to be the *continuity*, the finite both anchoring and riding on the *continuity*.

28. But let us go further: Waves riding on the ocean. The ocean impelled to make waves to express its nature. A "moment by moment" version of time is the creation of this *continuity's* cornucopia. Time and space themselves are the natural products of the reality of life and death—and its signature masterpiece.

29. As this freedom becomes no longer the hoped-for experience but the actuality, the voyager is free to be mortal and to help other mortals in a singular way.

30. This singular way is filled with tender poignancy allied with direct and unflinching awareness of what must be done. Again, in order to reach this stage, the voyager must have delved deeply into their own psychological needs and committed themselves to living an awakening life. Please note yet again, I say "awaken*ing*" because this effort never ceases. In fact, if it ceases, awakening has departed.

31. When all of this is so, then we can return to beauty in all its forms, including mandalas and symbolic signs of all kinds, but without the longing for what we might think they *point to* and *who they came from* and rather as things-in-themselves that may or may not point, but whose activity *is* their physical presence in the world of matter (which includes the world of spirit).

32. Color, vibrancy, steadiness, flow, pulsation, flexibility and courage are what we want to bring to our clients. To do so, we need to be involved with this ourselves.

33. From the point of view of the unhealed or un-matured ego, we lose everything. From the point of view of the healing ego, we lose everything in order to *find* everything. For the nondual voyager, losing and finding are the continuous activity of the *densities* and the vivid quality of the *continuity* itself. Both have a home.

34. Both are not "the spice of life" but what life is: spices—some acrid, some pleasant, some tasteless, and some even horrible.

35. From this position, we work to ease suffering, to bring rationality to our lives and the lives of people we work with.

36. True rationality is not "logical" any more than it is "illogical." It is an entirely different animal. It is pure cause and effect, which is to say, the interaction of the *densities* that make up the *continuity* and that take the simultaneity of *continuity* and *density* as a given fact. Cause and effect as a single thing.

37. To be truly rational is to be *for* life in its totality, to protect life at all times (within the context of our imperfections of course—which are part of life as well!), and to teach that the rational life is the most pleasurable and healing life.

38. To this end, the nondual voyager travels to every realm, finds him or herself under every leaf and within every stream, is blessed by the cold waters of spring and frozen waters of winter, bathes in heat and covers up in the cooling air when that comes.

39. No longer controlled by inner psychic movements, the nondual voyager—as much as possible, since we rise and fall and rise again!—is not a marionette but a dancer who engages in as many situations as possible, the spiraling and braided motions of life and death—to the benefit of all beings, past, present and even future.

Appendix Four: The Chain of Thought

1. As we learn to abide in the state of *continuity/density*, perhaps even making it our preferred vista of reality, our mental apparatus continues to be busy making connections, trying to discern patterns and figure conclusions.

2. In other words, we continue thinking.

3. This is a normal function of our minds, and if our minds are functioning normally and we are not having or attached to a particular (and self-limiting) "spiritual experience," this is bound to happen. Thinking is not the voyager/shaman's enemy—or the enemy of the nondual view.

4. If we are to include *thinking* as part of our broadened view of reality and not consider it an interloper that destroys the questionable pleasures of floating bodiless in the sensorium of pure *continuity without density*, the question then becomes: how do we use this built-in tendency to think in a way that is helpful to the nondual voyager?

5. To help us do that, I'd like to add the metaphor (or more accurately, a description) of another type of thinking I'll call the *chain of thought*.

6. This *chain of thought* becomes possible as we are committed to walking through the field of being with *bucolic mind*, an un-tense, panoramic mental state, being aware of *continuity/density*, and using other tools such as *hypnogogic awareness* and perception of

the *collage aspect* of reality, wherein the layered and overlapping aspects of reality constantly interact (some material, some seemingly non-material), reinterpreting the relationship and meaning of what we perceive. In this way, *our usual thinking process is free to become* the *chain of thought.*

7. Part of this differentiation from ordinary thinking is that an important ingredient in the *chain of thought* is the deep commitment to "unknowingness." This is to say, *we don't know what is important.*

8. We are not even "precociously thinking," that is, trying to figure out the world, but rather in a real sense letting the world figure *us* out as we handle ongoing thinking in a new way.

9. We are willing to let the complex fluxations of reality flow by, organizing themselves—and us!—as part of this process of voyaging.

10. Please note that this is not a passive, "allowing" process, but one we engage in with full conscious awareness. Activity in the world is an entirely different phenomenon when we participate rather than remain an observer who believes he or she is mythically sequestered. Instead: our watery body in the ocean, waving off the coast of Cape Cod—or from across the street in any town you happen to inhabit.

11. So thinking remains, as it should, but our relationship with it is changed.

12. Again, this is not a passive process but a dynamic one in which our attention and

focus, our ability to limit and control, are themselves seen as "other thoughts" contained in the greater set of thinking itself.

13. Regular thinking takes place in the arena of subject and object: we think about something and, most often, have a sense of a goal or objective. The subject-object split is maintained throughout this type of thought as a fundamental "flavor" even when one half of this equation—usually the subjective one—disappears, as in when we are *immersed* in thought so deeply that the thinker seems to become invisible and inhabits an indeterminate space, an abstract space in the "in-between."

14. Here we are in a *sort* of hypnogogic space—but one we are not fully conscious of. This space, when conscious, is useful for the voyager in other settings, but here we are not in it by choice.

15. *Chain of thought*, on the other hand, intensifies a physicalized, object-like sense of thought, even though thoughts themselves are intangible. There is a sense that *everything* can be thought, including the thinker. The thinker here is not a transcendent quasi-presence, an entity "united with air," or spaciousness itself, but is down to earth and has its hands and feet attached to everything it does.

16. There is a mistaken tendency among some spiritual seekers to think that to the extent that the viewer disappears, is submerged or invisible, the spiritual search is fulfilled, or the goal won. So from this point of view,

samadhi—the Hindu word that means complete non-thinking absorption in the moment—seems "higher" than other ordinary states.

17. But *chain of thought* denies that this is true. It includes *samadhi*—along with all other ordinary experiences—as the ground state of being. It is not interested in going anywhere but here. Its absorption is in whatever is happening rather than some idealized state.

18. But this *here* I am speaking about is infinite and extends, as I have said elsewhere in this book, infinitely in all directions.

19. When we favor one side over another, in this case, either the absolute or the relative, we are almost always doing so to protect ourselves from some sort of suffering. Either the world is too much with us, and we need the pseudo-rest of trying to live in the absolute alone—as if this were actually possible!—or, contrariwise, we find ourselves unable to leave the particular, where spaciousness itself feels like the enemy, as it reveals too much of our aloneness or emptiness.

20. Only when we learn to think in the state of true union, wherein neither the thinker nor his or her thoughts disappear, can we experience the usefulness and completeness of the *chain of thought*.

21. In the *chain of thought* approach, we allow our awareness itself to be part of the flux, another detail of reality, a precise linkage of associations we do not control but which

Exercise:
Allow all of your thoughts to flow freely while you are attentive—but not involved—in them. They are neither interesting nor uninteresting, insightful nor un-insightful. Instead, like any scene containing physical objects, these thoughts are "just there."

Now: let's equate "the thinker" with awareness itself. In other words, the thinker is not a "person" but pure awareness, a condition that allows you to be aware of the *chain of thoughts*.

Put this awareness "on the table" as well.

Now, everything is present: the thoughts as they pass by and even the awareness that lets you regard these thoughts and experience their presence.

Please stay in this space—awareness itself and the particular thoughts—from five to ten minutes in each session.

still mirror the deepest processes in our brains and chemistry along with our social and genetic makeup. We are assembled, just as, simultaneously, we are workers on the assembly line ourselves.

22. When I do this process as part of my voyaging, I have the experience of being able to follow a *chain of thought*, which for me is a picture of the person I am working with from their beginning until the present moment.

23. I do not hold this "picture" as a product that will give me "the answer." Instead, like all the elements of *continuity/density*, I accept it fully and then *let it organize me as I organize the session*.

24. In this way it becomes—as I am—a force in the universe, a world-line of not just time *but also of space*. In other words, this *chain of thought* takes up both dimensions simultaneously and not just one or the other.

> These thoughts are seen by the voyager as physical objects that endure. Thus, they have the dimension of time *and* space.

25. The inclusion of space here gives us precision and distance. The person's life is a single gesture, a nondual spiritual and bright object.

26. So, to contradict myself, I *do* achieve insight through this process, but the *quality* of this insight is more subtle, more *granular* than if I were simply using my mental processes (as in plain thinking) without the combination of all of these voyaging devices.

27. Doing things in this way ensures that what we get—the conclusions we come to, the

things we see that might help—are found in a way that is the most nondual and are not colored by a viewpoint we are not aware of, but one that includes the viewer and his or her viewpoint as part of the chain of associations and realizations.

28. All of this is very subtle. For example, doing this process as I have described it almost feels as if we are perusing the *Akashic* records, that is, the repository of all experience, related to a particular person.

29. The difference here, however, is that all of these processes change the person into a voyager. What this means is that the practitioner is lifted out of the astral realm, with its personal-*only* part-objects and unfinished emotional and psychic business seen as the only state of affairs, into the state of *continuity/density*, in which the impersonal helps to evolve the personal, and the personal makes the view of the impersonal—with all of its unfinished personal attributes included—possible.

The foundation for this level of insight is the practitioner themselves, practicing. Our ability to use this approach is completely tied to the experience we have of allowing the *chain of thought* and the awareness of thinking itself to exist together "on the table." *Chain of thought* is first and foremost a *personal practice*.

30. Our ideal state is the one in which the mutual co-arising of the absolute and relative exist as *functions of each other, rather than separate realms.*

31. Without this experience and understanding, the practitioner is always secretly fighting to make a safe harbor for themselves in the vastness of time and space *or* retreating to a safe distance—a position from which they can operate without having to challenge their own psychological makeup.

32. Nondual voyagers make no such frontiers.

33. The voyager who uses all of these tools is neither *here* nor *there*, is neither dead nor alive, to quote the Zen koan, and is in the nondual state from which the deepest creativity springs.

34. This *chain of thought* then becomes a universal moment, an ongoing spiritual object in space and time, the tender expression of an ongoing life.

35. The *chain of thought*, which itself is free from slavish attendance to personal psychology and stands equal to every other object in the universe, makes us free to participate and interact with reality—ours, our clients', the world itself—in a new and fresh way. We are able to stand in the field and reap the ripe crop, turning all of *continuity/density* into a handful of food we can share with someone else.

Coda

The whole concept of being in the Now has serious problems. And more important than the misconceptions about what the Now actually is, this incorrect temporal concept is a needless obstruction to spiritual understanding.

The Now does not and cannot exist in the condition we call "life." No matter how you slice it, we are always—even in the very best of circumstances—a micro- or nanosecond from actually being here now. Nerve impulses are not immediate, though they are designed to portray that illusion. According to psychologist David Myers:[*]

> *Depending on the type of fiber, the neural impulse travels at speed ranging from a sluggish 2 miles per hour to, in some myelinated fibers, a breakneck 200 or more miles per hour. But even this top speed is 3 million times slower than the speed of electricity through a wire.*

This means that between touching and feeling touch, depending upon your frame of reference, a small lifetime of duration exists.

In addition, there is the speed of light to consider. Although light is very, very fast, it takes a finite moment of time for the light bouncing off an object to reach our retina and then, to register via our optical nerve in our brain. We are already in the past and perhaps even contemplating the future outcome of what we are seeing.

So we are always a little bit out of the Now. Never in the Now, never can be in the Now. And this is all for the good.

My own research has shown me that consciousness arises essentially because different areas of the brain are running on slightly off-set clocks and that this off-set is responsible not only

---

[*] David G. Myers, *Psychology*, Worth Publishing, 2004.

for consciousness but for the feeling of identity as well. In other words, the brain is not a unified temporal environment with all of its parts running on the same clock, but one that has several different rates of times running at once, some faster, some slower. This is how consciousness arises: one part has to be in a slightly different time and space to see, relate and react to the other. Each part can "observe" the other being separate in both time and space, as tiny as those differences are. Perhaps we will find that consciousness depends upon quantum phenomena—in which case these seemingly minute differences in time will make Grand Canyons of difference.

This condition of temporal and spatial difference allows self-consciousness to arise.

Further, I have noticed that if the timing is too far apart, the consequence is someone whose identity (self-consciousness) is too vague, too permeable, too unsteady. Their sense of self is diffuse. In extreme cases, the center cannot hold; the person's identity can be extremely fragile.

Conversely, a person whose brain has timings that are too exact, too close together, can become rigidly involved in the subject-object world, which is to say, someone who rigidly adheres to the physical world and a strict and limited interpretation of their sensory data in order to decide what is true or not true. Probably most of our brains have combinations of these timing preferences, making our identities more malleable than we normally think they are.

The implications for both of these types of "timing" and the types of identities and concurrent world-views they create—based on this sense of identity that is created as the parts of the brain notice each other in different ways—are profound. These of course are currently generalizations and need more research.

While thinking about all of this, it further occurred to me that only the dead are in the Now, that the very act of leaving conscious life, of no longer having the ability to offset or even create a sensorium in time, as it were, creates a type of consciousness that has no identity, that has no self (since "self" is a concept you only get by looking at something that is not the self) and consequently, has no self-reflection—even though the raw materials of consciousness may still be present. We could say that the type of consciousness that exists in the actual Now has absolutely no self-reflection. It cannot know itself.

However, since nothing is pure in nature, even something that has no self-reflection must contain, on some level, its opposite, in exactly the same way that the Heisenberg principle suggests that even a vacuum must be the home of virtual particles that blink on and off. In other words, even a vacuum is not empty. So it is with death: this no-self state of death must also give rise simultaneously, by virtue of its existence, to life, to consciousness, to the re-birth of self, to the pairing of structures of some sort— perhaps on the quantum level—that allow for these temporal and spatial differences and which therefore, lead to self-conscious life.

Nondual voyaging allows the voyager to get very, very close to non-self-reflection state, yet remain in the land of the living. We could say that nondual voyaging operates in the borderline between these worlds, close enough to apprehend the presence of the dead as they leave life and the presence of life as it leaves death. The nondual voyager lives and works in that dream state— that non-trance, utterly clear, dream state—where all of this is possible. We are floating with our feet on the ground. Are we alive or dead? It is impossible to know. The implications here go way beyond the dead and make comprehensible how the voyager can partake of many levels of subtle quasi-phenomena. We live in the non-binary place where life and death are not opposites, a life within the *continuity/density*.

Are we skeleton or sage? We cannot know. So we use our time to bow to everyone and everything. A complete mystery surrounds our being in every direction. All the living and all the dead are in us at this very moment. Every dimension and phenomenon, in us right now. And everything is precious, every enlargement of our understanding an opening into more territory into which our hearts can reach. We are the benefactors of a life well-lived and since this one heart—our own—is also the heart of every sentient being, everyone applauds.

Acknowledgements

Many, many people deserve thanks for the existence of this book. I do not know the names of many of them since they exist in a sort of in-between place, the cloud of unknowing that accompanies all of us who grow up in this world. The inhabitants of this cloud are nameless because we have never met them physically. They are not of this time or place. And yet they are, carried here over the rough and smooth dimensions by the mysteries of time in this pulsating universe. Some people are lucky—through no special effort on their own part—that these ghosts come to visit and even take up residence in order to help in the task of clarifying the great questions of human life and human healing. I see them in this waking dream I call a life, and I did nothing special to deserve them but invite them in. And even the ability to invite was given to me gratis by some wheeling kindness that sometimes shows itself in our personal time and space.

And then there are others whose names I know: My wife, Arlene Shulman, without whom I would be lost in my own hall of mirrors without a heart to lead me out; Stephanie Ross and Deb Sprague, who kindly made a space in their little Cape Cod space for me to write serenely; my wonderful and talented cohorts Tom Schneider, Jeff Casper, Nancy Yeilding, Kim Burnham, Shelah Stein and Tove Borgendale, all of whom helped finalize the manuscript in the form you have in your hands. I also deeply thank the anonymous donors whose generosity made the Jason Shulman Library possible. May blessings drift down to them from Heaven! And, finally, to my students, for whom this is written. We are all studying hard to be awakening healers. May we all accomplish our task!

About the Author

Jason Shulman is an American spiritual teacher whose original work springs from his Judaic and Buddhist background. He is the founder of *A Society of Souls: The School for Nondual Healing and Awakening (ASOS)*, based in the United States, Europe, and the United Arab Emirates. Through ASOS he teaches the distinctive body of nondual work he has developed to awaken the human spirit: Nondual Healing, Impersonal Movement and the Work of Return. Jason's main concern has been to develop paths of healing the mind, body and spirit based on his own understanding of the difficulties inherent in the human condition. Through his studies and practice, Jason has developed a unique perspective on human consciousness and the nature of existence. His work seeks to translate this perspective into a replicable and clearly-delineated path for other seekers of truth to follow. He has been especially interested in applying personal spiritual work to methods of transforming society at large. To that end, he has created the MAGI Process, a nondual method of working with conflicts between people, institutions and governments. He is the author of numerous monographs and books, and several albums of his work as a singer and songwriter. More about his work can be found at www.societyofsouls.com

The Foundation for Nonduality is dedicated to making the principles of nondual thinking and practice, as articulated by Jason Shulman, available to the greater public. The Foundation's purpose is to transform the consciousness of individuals in order to help alleviate suffering in the world. All proceeds from the sale of this book go to support the work of The Foundation for Nonduality (www.nonduality.us.com).

THE FOUNDATION
FOR NONDUALITY

Made in United States
North Haven, CT
29 May 2023

37127283R00174